D0109354

SEASONS
OF
FRIENDSHIP

SEASONS
OF
FRIENDSHIP

Naomi and Ruth as a Pattern

By
Marjory Zoet Bankson

San Diego, California

LuraMedia™

Also by Marjory Zoet Bankson:
Braided Streams: Esther and a Woman's Way of Growing
Braided Streams Tape: Marjory Zoet Bankson Tells the Story of Esther

© Copyright 1987 LuraMedia
San Diego, California
International Copyright Secured
Publisher's Catalog Number LM-607
Printed and Bound in the United States of America

LuraMedia
P.O. Box 261668
10227 Autumnview Lane
San Diego, CA 92126-0998

Library of Congress Cataloging-in-Publication Data

Bankson, Marjory Zoet.

    Seasons of friendship.

    Bibliography: p.
      1. Ruth (Biblical character) 2. Naomi (Biblical character)
3. Friendship—Biblical teaching. 4. Bible. O.T. Ruth—Criticism,
interpretation, etc. I. Title.
BS580.R8B36   1987   222'.3506   87-32528
ISBN 0-931055-41-5

All Scripture quotations unless otherwise noted are taken from the Holy Bible, NEW INTERNATIONAL VERSION. Copyright © 1973, 1978, 1984 by International Bible Society. Used by permission.

The Scripture quotations identified JB are from THE JERUSALEM BIBLE, copyright © 1964 by Darton, Longman & Todd, Ltd. and Doubleday, a division of Bantam, Doubleday, Dell Publishing Group, Inc. Reprinted by permission of the publisher.

The Scripture quotations identified RSV are from the REVISED STANDARD VERSION BIBLE, copyright 1946, 1952, 1971 by the Division of Christian Education of the National Council of the Churches of Christ in the USA. Used by permission.

*To all my friends, named and unnamed,
who have enriched my life,
especially my sisters, Mimi and Barbara,
who were my earliest friends.*

Contents

"Ruth and Naomi"
Walnut sculpture by Sister Helena Steffens-meier, SSSF
Alverno College, Milwaukee, Wisconsin

Invitation

We live in a promiscuous culture in which the quiet support of committed friendship goes largely unnoticed. Yet we long to be known, understood, and received without conditions, so we move from person to person, group to group, looking for a place to be loved. We search for a perfect mate, or we compromise ourselves in a harmful relationship, because we are afraid that no one can really accept the full range of who we are.

In our transient society we tend to ignore or compromise the very friendships that can support a primary relationship: a marriage, a job, or a specially-bonded relationship with a parent or child. Without friends, however, even our primary relationships lose their quality because we lose our capacity to sustain a sole relationship. Without friends, we lose touch with our humanity. The friends who provide space for our individuality—and companionship for the *loneliness* created by that individuality—also provide a context for self-identity that is essential to being truly alive.

The trouble is that close friendships are hard to nurture and even harder to keep in our transient world. Most of us have learned more about losing friends by moving away than we know about finding new ones or about deepening the friendships we have. I thought that marriage would solve the problem—that I would marry Peter Bankson and have a friend for life. I do have a friend in Peter, but that friendship is not enough! I have discovered that different seasons in my life require different kinds of friendship and different levels of companionship. For many of us, learning how to love a friend is more complex than finding an ideal mate!

This book is about friendship and about being a friend, but there is no advice or easy formula here. Rather I have taken the biblical story of Ruth and Naomi as a polarizing lens through which we can look at our lives as contemporary women. Through the story of these two ancient women, I hope to bring focus and clarity to some of the dynamics that assist or hinder friendship.

The connection between my own search for a close friend and the biblical story of Ruth began quite unconsciously, twenty-five years ago. Like many other couples of our generation, Peter and I used Ruth's pledge to Naomi as the basis for our marriage vows: "Where you go, I will go." We didn't think much about the relationship between Naomi and Ruth which lay behind this vow; we never discussed how one-sided Ruth's promise was. Because it was my role to shape the wedding ceremony, I just chose Ruth's pledge as the ideal statement of my own intention to give up my past for our future together. As we turned from the altar, the minister read Ruth's pledge:

"Whither thou goest, I will go;
and where thou lodgest, I will lodge:
thy people shall be my people,
thy God, my God."   (Ruth 1:16 KJV)

The statement was true for us, and it still describes the intent of our marriage, but the process of going and lodging and finding "our people" and discovering the nature of God has been varied and difficult, rich and rewarding. The process has brought me back to the story of Ruth and Naomi with different eyes. I now see that God's story, as it is revealed in the lives of Ruth and Naomi, is a story of friendship after the conventional supports of marriage and family are stripped away by death. It is a story of how two women began to experience God's presence in a way that gave them value and worth—at a time when the culture regarded women as property and mere incubators for children. The Book of Ruth is also a parable of God with us in daily life, of God as friend.

Historically, the story is set in the period before David's monarchy, in the time "when the Judges ruled," about 1100 B.C. Defined as a people by their monotheism and covenant relationship with Yahweh, the Hebrews had gained control of the highlands on the west side of the Dead Sea following their exodus from Egypt. Yahweh was generally pictured as a male warrior and judge during that period; the Book of Ruth introduces another view of God that is more female and relational.

Biblical scholars generally agree that the Book of Ruth was actually written in the the post-exile period of Ezra and Nehemiah, when the issue of cultural and religious purity was part of re-establishing Israel's identity (fifth century B.C.). Some authors say that Ruth was written to counter the campaign against marrying foreign women. I see a prophetic theme in Ruth, a theme which values women as people and opens the covenant to all people who are called to faith in God. Ruth presages the vision of shalom that Jesus lived five centuries later.

Traditionally, Ruth's story has been associated with the Feast of Weeks, which marked the spring grain harvest or the "first fruits" (Exodus 23:14-17, Exodus 34:22, Deuteronomy 16:9-12). On the surface, the connection is obvious: food was provided for Ruth and Naomi after a period of search and famine. The Feast of Weeks was also known as Pentecost because it was celebrated fifty days after Passover as a remembrance of Moses receiving the law. By association with Pentecost or the Feast of Weeks, the story of Ruth presents the spirit behind the Law in a radical way.

Elements of Naomi's faith and Ruth's commitment echo Moses' faith and the Exodus story, although the female figures stand in shocking contrast in their courage and simplicity: Naomi and Ruth had no burning bush, no manna in the desert, no pillar of flame, and no promise of final security, yet they undertook a desert journey toward the promised land. Given the period and the patriarchal bias of fifth century Israel, it is startling to see God's presence and purpose embodied by these two women. Their friendship implies a larger purpose for women than bearing children and a more inclusive loving God than the Exodus story reveals. If Moses led a people to external freedom and identity, Naomi and Ruth lead us to an internal promised land of spiritual wholeness and integration.

The translation of Ruth's name provides a focus on friendship and a connection with the nature of God as friend. One source quotes the Hebrew root for Ruth, *rut*, as a contraction meaning "lady friend(s)."* Another identifies Ruth as a

---

*John L. McKenszie, S.J., *Dictionary of the Bible*.

Moabite word connected with the verb *ra'ah*, meaning "shep-herding a flock," denoting "to associate with" and connoting "friend or friendship."* Both sources point to friendship as the core issue in Ruth's name and, therefore, as the central theme in this story of Pentecost.

Since Pentecost has further been transformed by Christ-ians—from a festival celebrating the receipt of the Law fifty days after Passover, into the coming of the Holy Spirit to the early church some fifty days after Easter—we can look at the story of Naomi and Ruth with new eyes: perhaps the most common way that we experience the empowering presence of God's spirit is through special friendships!

Early in the story, Naomi pronounced a crucial command to Ruth and Orpah: "Go back to your mother's house!" Even for us today, at the beginning of every woman's spiritual journey, the decision to leave our "mother's house" is the beginning of mature self-identity. We do it in layers, again and again. As we let Naomi's challenge resound inwardly, we may need to go back to "our mother's house" because we are not ready to leave that security behind, or because there is unfinished business to be completed. Some of us need to examine the choice and decide, as Ruth did, that it is time to leave the past behind and make a commitment to friendship without knowing where it will lead. Some of us will have to stand in Naomi's place, bereft of all past security, willing to risk everything for a rumor of hope that seems far away in the future.

The image of seasons in friendship has emerged out of my reflections on the story of Naomi and Ruth. Each season in nature has its own character: sometimes the distinctions are subtle, as in the Pacific Northwest where I grew up; sometimes the contrasts are extreme, as in Alaska where I lived when I was first married. Each season of friendship gives rise to new life for one or both partners, as it did for these biblical women—as spring to a frozen land.

It is no accident that the hopeful message of Easter resurrection comes in spring or that Pentecost marks the shift

---

*Carole Rayburn, "Three Women from Moab," *Spinning a Sacred Yarn.*

toward summer. The overlay of nature and religious celebrations takes on additional meaning when we can find those same patterns in our own lives. The spiral of seasons provides an image of faith development that can reveal places where we are stuck or may have a special need. I hope that the metaphor of seasons will reveal some of the richness in the story of Naomi and Ruth and in your own friendships.

Throughout the book I have included examples from my own life as a model for ways in which you might find the spirit of these biblical women in your friendships. The exercise of doing the journal questions for each section is designed to help you bring your own life story to the pattern of friendship between Ruth and Naomi. Sharing your answers to the journal questions with others in an attitude of prayer and openness can take the reflection process one step further, toward healing the past and energizing the future.

I hope that you will use the questions inserted throughout to build new friendships. . .and a new fabric for our transient society. By telling our own stories, we can open our lives to God and to the community of other seekers. The process will gradually reach back in time, so we can learn to love those parts of our lives that seem unacceptable today; we may be able to love those parts of our early lives that seem to threaten us with bondage or hurt. We can even learn to name and love our internal enemies, although we may never like them. I dream of a time when the churches on every corner can be a place for discovering friends to bless our lives with acceptance and interest, with commitment and support. In that company we can share the journey of faithful people everywhere.

Before you begin, take a few minutes and read the story of Ruth as it is found in any translation of the Bible.

— *Marjory Zoet Bankson*

1. Circle of Seasons

Spring
    season of "we"
        of nurture and feeding
        husband and wife
        mother and child
        best friends at the well together.

Summer
    season of "I"
        of hunger and search
        leaving home
        for hope of finding food
        in a foreign land.

Autumn
    season of "us"
        of harvest and community
        rules and rituals
        a matrix of family and friends
        with stories of past and future.

    Ten years Naomi waited
    for a future to be born
        to Ruth (the beloved)
        and Orpah (she who turns away)
            but no children came
    then death claimed her sons.

Winter
    season of "me"
        of solitude and silence
        drawing on reserves
        dimly seen.

Numbed by events that took her hope away,
Naomi chose life
>   *a journey home*
>   *around the Dead Sea*
to die or. . .see spring come again.

Spring: Season of "We"

Spring is the season of birth, of sharing the newborn parts of adult life with a mothering friend. The primary image of mother and child is full of hope, of possibilities, and of unknowns that will unfold with time. In adult relationships spring is a season for temporary dependence, nourishment, and protection of tender new growth.

The biblical story of Naomi and Ruth began just beyond the promise of springtime, but the setting of Naomi's preparation for friendship can be derived from clues in the text. A young couple, Naomi and Elimelech, were already married and had been blessed with two children, both sons. Husband and wife had become "one flesh" within the Hebrew understanding of marriage (Genesis 2:24), and their budding family was regarded as a sign of God's special favor. The promise of spring in nature had already been realized, and they had every reason to rejoice. Naomi, whose name meant "pleasant," and Elimelech, whose name meant "my god is king," seemed like the perfect young couple as their family expanded. In Naomi's words, she was "full" (1:21).*

The natural division of labor in a Jewish village made it possible for women to nurture and support each other. Their homes were close, their work communal, their families large. Many tasks were shared in such a village: getting water,

---

*Unless specified, all Scripture references are from the Book of Ruth, New International Version.

washing clothes, preparing food, spinning and weaving. . . rhythmic activities that provided a setting for sharing the lore of women. Female friendships would have happened naturally around these common tasks in a rural village, without the need for any special pledge or commitment.

Since women were expected to marry and have children, having two sons would have given Naomi a place of honor and respect in the family-oriented circle of Hebrew women living in Bethlehem. Naomi would have formed a dyadic bond with each of her sons and perhaps with a best friend among the young mothers of Bethlehem as well. Her springtime friendships would have included the sharing of excitement about new marriages and pregnancies, and the joining in household tasks centered around growing families.

Although we do not know if Naomi had a special friend during this early period of joyful abundance, we can guess that she might have from her name—"pleasant" or "sweet"—and from the obvious welcome that the women gave her when she returned to Bethlehem as an older woman (1:19). However, if women did form special friendships within the context of village life, that fact was not generally recorded. Women were not regarded as carriers of God's truth. That cultural bias makes the story of Ruth and Naomi extraordinarily important because the presence of God is revealed in the unfolding relationship between the two women.

Naomi's preparation for her part in their relationship was clearly mainstream and conventional: she identified herself primarily as a wife and mother. Since Naomi would have left her childhood home and moved in with Elimelech's family (leaving her own mother's house for that of her mother-in-law), she probably sought the friendship of another young woman in that household to ease her loneliness and newness there, but her friendships with other women would always have taken second place to her responsibilities as a wife.

A network of women in which we can find spring friends to share the newborn parts of our lives is probably more difficult for us to find than it was for Naomi. We live and work as individuals, family units are small and often transient, and in our effort to become independent, we often feel ambivalent about spring friends because we are ashamed to need mothering as adults. Until recently, very little has been written about the importance of female friendships in adult stages of development.

For many women, marriage holds the promise of spring friendship with a spouse. Over time, however, a married couple may not be able to provide the nurturing for each other that is needed. In a traditional marriage, the wife is socialized to provide emotional support while depending on her husband's financial support, but she may not receive enough nurturing back from him to help her make the shift from being an independent, single person to being a wife and mother.

The time when we are separating from our biological mothers in an effort to set up a new home and family may be the very time when we feel the need for guidance or support of a mothering person. The money and sex that usually come with marriage are not a substitute for emotional nurturing. To get that emotional care, a woman often needs a female friend—a spring friend—to companion her into marriage and to support the role changes brought about by marriage. And if a woman has not really separated from her own parents prior to marriage, she may need the emotional support of a spring friend even more! Single women, too, need mothering at the same stage of setting up a separate household, but they may find it easier to seek a spring friend for care and support than a newly married woman.

The presence of a mothering friend is often signaled by food: sharing meals is a mother-child equivalent of the sexual intimacy one might have with a man. If we understand that all adults—men and women—go through periods of dependency and a need for emotional nurturing when a new stage or part of one's self is being born, then we do not have to be afraid of needing such care. Spring friends are natural and normal when we move into a new situation or take on a new challenge, when something new is being born in our lives.

When I consider the seasons of Naomi's adult life and the

friendships she probably had as a young mother in Bethlehem, I am surprised by the similarity my story seems to have with hers. Peter and I were married soon after we graduated from college, and we moved to Alaska for his first Army assignment. In Fairbanks I taught junior high history and English, and he was a lieutenant in an infantry company. Our closest friends were two other young couples in exactly the same circumstances: the wives were teachers, and the husbands were lieutenants in different Army units.

When the men were "in the field" for training, Olga, Dee, and I would often get together to grade papers, read, knit, or just talk (there was no television in Fairbanks then). We reached out for companionship and intellectual stimulation from each other, and we shared practical information and fun time, too. One to one, we shared some of the disappointments of married life, but generally we cushioned for each other the loneliness of being in a new place by providing encouragement and emotional support. We were far from home, as we still thought of the combination of place and parents that we came from: home was not yet Alaska. Having children seemed to be the key factor in creating a real home of our own, but none of us had children yet. We created a common history by telling about our siblings and parents, and we created a new family of adults by spending holidays together as couples. My spring friends Olga and Dee helped me adjust to a new world of being "a dependent," literally and figuratively.

Olga, Dee, and I acted like adults (most of the time). We shared the externals of making a home, but inside, I felt lost and alone. I suspect the others did, too. We mothered each other, sharing stories and experiences, along with the food and outdoor adventure of a frontier land. We entertained each other on meager budgets and laughed a lot together. Those springtime friends were essential to me because they cared for the lonely child inside of me at a time when I needed to appear competent and capable of being a grown woman to my husband and the Army community in which we lived.

> **Journal Questions**
> **Spring: Season of "We"**
>
> - When and where did you establish your first home?
>
> - Did you have a close woman friend who shared that experience with you? How would you describe her?
>
> - What did you do together that felt nurturing?

Summer: Season of "I"

With the same inevitability that the seasons in nature come round with the sun, internal or external changes take us from spring friendships into summer. Idealism gives way to practical realities, and we tire of the very things that once fed us. Individually, we begin to hunger for something more. Relationally, the cozy intimacy of "we" gives way to open spaces and different activities that help us achieve separate identities: an assertive "I" emerges. Summer friends are less nurturing, more distinct and functional, and more stimulating than spring friends. Summer friends call forth initiative, individuality, and independence.

In the biblical story the shift from spring to summer for Naomi came slowly over several years as the juiciness of spring gave way to hardened soil and sun-baked days of summer. Famine stalked the land and threatened the Israelites with death. Some stayed in Bethlehem, hoping for a sign of Yahweh's covenant promise once again. Others left to look elsewhere for sustenance. When Elimelech and Naomi decided to leave the promised land, they also left the implied "we" of the covenant. They decided to depend on their own resources rather than wait for a miracle. They separated from past securities of land and people and God to establish control over their own lives by leaving Bethlehem.

Pared down to the bare essentials, Naomi and Elimelech walked away from the promise of Yahweh's protection, risking their lives for survival. They traveled away from their homeland in Judah, around the Dead Sea to the land of Moab, repeating the Exodus journey in reverse toward some hoped-for future in their personal lives. They left the protective and nurturing promise of the covenant. The young couple had to rely on their own wits and trust the presence of God to go beyond the laws and customs of their past because there was no earthly authority to provide them with safe passage. Their Dead Sea journey was a choice for independence, for a summer relationship with God as well as with human friends.

When they arrived in Moab, Naomi had to find ways to make a new home in a foreign language among the Moabite women. That called for strength her mother had never needed, for skills she had never learned in Bethlehem. Somehow she was able to make that transition without the supportive network of the women who had mothered her in Bethlehem. Naomi and Elimelech succeeded in making a place in Moab, finding ways to live and work while both sons grew, but the difficulty and separateness of their life in Moab was symbolized by the fact that there were no more children.

For a decade or more, they defined the boundaries of their Hebrew family among strangers. Elimelech's name, which meant "my god is king," conveyed his continuing allegiance to Yahweh. The young Hebrew family probably continued their own religious practices within the household and remained aliens among the people of Moab. As Naomi toughened her pleasantness into purpose, she no longer needed mothering. Survival and separateness clarified her character, defined her identity as a Hebrew woman alone in a foreign land. Yet Naomi must have found enough support during those long years in Moab to make it home to her. Her summer friends were those who could meet her strength with theirs.

Leaving home and claiming the separateness of "I" from the inevitable fusion of a family (childhood or adult) marks the season of summer for our own friendships. When we reach beyond the comforts of home, of known roles and religion, toward an unknown summertime landscape, then we reach for friends who will meet us in our travels and cause us to stretch for something more . . . something far away, even alien. External restlessness usually signals an internal change. We may feel hungry or thirsty, even when there is enough literal food for sustenance. Indeed, we may try to fill that spiritual hunger with physical food and notice that we are gaining (or losing) weight during an intense summer period.

For some, an internal summer season comes when children grow up and mothers begin to ask, "What's next?" For others, marriages dry into routines and jobs lose their challenge. We begin to search the bookshelves for other people's stories to stretch our minds or disturb our souls. And those solitary figures cross our paths with strangeness, reach out a dry hand, or meet our glance with a piercing glare. Summer friends come singly, not in pairs.

Summer means finding a way to live in a strange land. It means strengthening ego boundaries and forging ahead with an inner will, rather than depending upon approval or support from a mothering figure. A summer friend is more partner than parent. My own summertime friends have called me beyond the conventional safety of marriage and teaching. Each one has challenged me to find a new language of expression and a new structure for offering my gifts.

After two years of teaching in Alaska, I decided to go back to school for graduate study in history. I was longing for something to fill the terrible hunger and thirst for . . . what? I told myself that I wanted something more to feed my mind than teaching eighth-graders, but I knew I also felt a thirst for some other kind of community, for books and for the arid world of ideas instead of the fleshy reality of so many people living close together on the Army post. Perhaps, too, I was experiencing an end to my romantic dream that marriage would complete me without further inner work (I didn't even know there was such a thing then). My inner world developed a stormy kind of loneliness, fed by books and ideas, crackling with energy.

Through a connection from my college roommate, I met a summer friend. Sheila was teaching economics at the University of Alaska. This tall Jewish woman from New York embodied difference in Fairbanks, challenging the values implied by Peter's Army career with her anti-war remarks, and inviting my friendship out of her own loneliness. Her questions helped me to find language for my own opinions, and her presence validated an intellectual part of my life that was submerged in the homey closeness of my spring friendships. Sheila was obviously different from me, and that helped me to identify my own boundaries, to experience myself as "I" instead of part of a "we."

As a summertime friend, Sheila did not stay in my life as part of the pattern of friends who have continued to sustain my sense of self. Perhaps summer friends are more likely to connect deeply and then slip out of our lives because they are not rooted in an on-going community. Instead, summer friends are likely to be solitary figures who meet us at critical times of stretching boundaries and risking beyond the safe dyads of spring. Summer friends belong to a particular time and place, at the edge of one's known past, calling forth unique differences, righting the balance between pairing and person.

Journal Questions
Summer: Season of "I"

- Identify a period in your life when you shifted from spring to summer.

- Name a friend who shared that summer season of search, hungering, or new definition of yourself.

- How did this summer friend differ from your spring friend? How did your summer relationship differ from your spring relationship?

Autumn: Season of "Us"

In nature, autumn is the time to harvest what has been sown in the spring and ripened by summer sun. Fall harvest is a communal activity, a time of "us," a time of sorting and storing. If there has been enough rain to balance summer's heat and light, then autumn brings harvest, food, and celebration rituals for a whole community. If there has not been enough water, food is scarce and the drought of summer creates an element of fear about survival through the coming winter. This is true inside as well as out, in our souls as well as in nature.

In life, autumn is a time for gathering what was begun earlier. We join with others in the harvesting process, and we find nourishment in communal activities. A former spring friendship may suddenly mature as the nurturing qualities of a special twosome are spread out to include other people, and a singular summer friendship may be integrated into one's community as the number of connections expand. If summer is a period of independence and search, then fall is a time of interdependence and storing away, a season to celebrate the richness of different people coming together—a season of "us."

By the time her sons were grown, Naomi apparently felt at home in Moab, but her roots there must have been tested when her husband, Elimelech, died. At that point, she might have returned to her homeland in Bethlehem in order for her sons Mahlon and Chilion to marry Hebrew women. Instead, she remained in Moab where her two sons married foreign wives, Ruth and Orpah. Naomi's decision to stay was a rejection of both her childhood home and the cultural values of her people. She chose her own way instead, whether by asserting her will or by giving in to the wishes of her sons, who would not have remembered Bethlehem except through the stories told by Naomi and Elimelech.

According to the biblical story, Naomi's autumn period lasted for ten years. Although the fruits of her life seemed meager as the years passed and no grandchildren were born, Naomi did not weaken in her resolve or abandon her Moab home. Naomi's hope and faith lay with living sons who could provide an economic base for the family and a future *if* they had children.

Naomi may have felt like a stranger in her own house with sons who spoke as Moabites and with Elimelech, her partner through so many trials, now gone. Could Ruth and Orpah be called friends for Naomi? There were obvious language and cultural differences between a mother who spoke Hebrew and belonged to the covenantal faith of Moses and Yahweh, and two young women who were living in the cultural milieu of their own land and people. But Ruth and Orpah belonged to Naomi's household and must have developed some sense of common purpose with her, even if they could not be thought of as friends.

As the heart of her small family in Moab, Naomi was still very much identified with the role of being a mother, but her role had a different quality because she was also the head of her household. The names of her sons, which meant "sickness" and "pining away," suggested that they were not strong male figures who could take over the role of their father. Naomi's autumn years were a time of consolidating her power, stabilizing her relationships with her daughters-in-law, and establishing her own kind of spiritual leadership within the family.

As the years went by, Naomi's family would have developed a sense of "us" as separate from the society in which they lived. To sustain her hope, Naomi probably returned to some of the roles and traditions that sustained her first separation from her mother's home, finding community in the shared tasks of women's work and comfort in the stories of Yahweh's provision for the Israelites as they lived in the desert between Egypt and the promised land.

In our own day, we also seek community by returning to the customs and rituals of our parents. When we talk about our place of origin, we usually name the town in which we grew up—our first experience of community beyond the family. As adults, we often need to leave that home in order to find a new place of belonging, but we do not leave our need for community. We look for a group of people who will accept and value our individual differences, as well as provide enough intimacy to make us feel welcome. The simple fact of language suggests that humans are created for community and for communicating with each other. We begin to find community in a new place by returning to or creating a common body of images and interpretive stories.

Our autumn friends belong to a community matrix of relationships surrounding the immediate home and family. For some, that means an extended family; for others, a church community; for still others, a network of individuals spread across the country who can be supportive by phone, letters, and an occasional visit. Those autumn friends whose words and deeds touch something deeper than the surface become part of "us." It is only in community that we learn the deeper lessons of loving those who are not like ourselves.

In our first cycle of seasons as adults, Peter and I looked for autumn community among the people who clustered around our special interests: books and conversation, camping and photography. We tried to create community around our dinner table by inviting diverse friends from the university and the Army post. At Christmas and Easter, we made a special effort to include others who might also be feeling lonely and far from home. For an evening, at least, we could share the harvest of our lives.

As my spring and summer friends moved away from Alaska and graduate school shifted my focus from teaching to learning, I reached out to a new community of friends who shared my interests at the university. One friend emerged from the cluster of couples whom we liked. Ann was in a book club with me, and we deepened our friendship when she became the editor of a small literary magazine for which I was writing. Her interests and education were similar to mine, and when each of our mothers visited Alaska, Ann and I found some additional background connections. Culturally, Ann was sophisticated and unpretentious. Like me, she was interested in having friends beyond the Army post, in town and at the university. She entertained easily, so the circle of interesting people to share dinner with actually grew through our particular friendship.

Although our relationship was not as intense as my earlier spring pairings, Ann is still part of my support network today while the others are not. Perhaps autumn friendships are preserved over time because autumn interactions thrive in a community of home and work, and include a spiritual dimension.

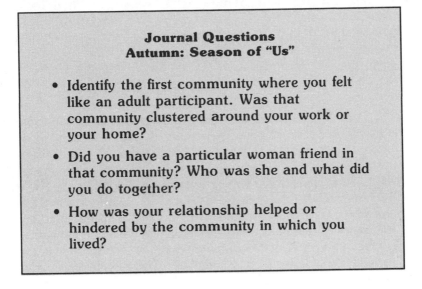

Journal Questions
Autumn: Season of "Us"

- Identify the first community where you felt like an adult participant. Was that community clustered around your work or your home?

- Did you have a particular woman friend in that community? Who was she and what did you do together?

- How was your relationship helped or hindered by the community in which you lived?

Winter: Season of "Me"

The transition from autumn to winter usually comes with a crisis, descending like a deadening chill or a sudden freeze. When winter comes as a season of friendship, we move away from others and go deep inside, to focus on "me." Like hibernating animals, we burrow within ourselves and withdraw from more "friendly friends," choosing those who walk best in silence. Winter is a time for solitude and commitment to inward leadings.

Naomi's extended family in Moab waited for children to be born to Ruth and Mahlon, Orpah and Chilion, but no children came. The close of Naomi's autumn years were marred by the bitter realization that her childless sons carried some kind of curse: even their names—"sickness" and "pining away"—suggested illness or blight. With no sign of children, there may have been increasing alienation from the fertility-worshipping culture in Moab. Autumn faded into winter as Naomi's two sons sickened and died.

Naomi faced the winter season of her life with none of her family to comfort her. She was an old woman without any future. Like many women who identify themselves solely with the role of being wife and mother, Naomi considered that her useful life was finished. It looked as if Yahweh had abandoned her in a foreign country and cursed her family with barrenness, taking away the only promise of life after death that the Hebrews recognized.

Then Naomi heard that God had visited her own people in Bethlehem, bringing food. Frozen with grief and stunned by her losses, she set her face toward her homeland. Her decision was an act of will. She simply refused to give up, although all the external signs of life were negative. Her decision probably grew out of the independence she had gained during her summer years and the spiritual consolidating that she had done during her autumn period in Moab. When the word came that Yahweh had visited her people, she had the faith to believe that Yahweh would not turn against her if she went back. Her decision to return to her place of birth was an act of courage.

With Ruth and Orpah alongside her, Naomi started toward Bethlehem on foot. In some ways she was retracing her summer journey with Elimelech from Bethlehem to Moab, but instead of two young sons, Naomi had two mature daughters-in-law with her, and there was no man for comfort or protection. Naomi was in charge. Although traveling with others, she was alone inside.

The three widows walking beside the Dead Sea epitomized winter. Wrapped in silence, they moved slowly away from Moab toward Bethlehem, without any star to guide them except Naomi's memory and her will. Cold, alone and hungry, the promise of food was both an inner and an outer beacon. Dim hope was enough to feed Naomi's soul as her tough old body plodded across the desert, one step at a time.

Death marked the shift into winter for Naomi as it does for each one of us today. As a season of friendship, winter comes when we turn from extroverted relationships in community to an introverted focus on self and survival. It can happen when a community is suddenly taken away, as it was for Naomi. It can happen through a change in health or economic circumstances, job, or home setting. Winter withdrawal may also happen simply because we are creatures sensitive to darkness and light, cold and warmth, and our souls need a time to rest and renew from the inside out. Winter friends wait together, connecting in silence around some small source of warmth or hope.

In my own life, winter came when we moved from Alaska to Georgia because of Peter's Army career. Leaving graduate school was a severe blow: my course work was done, comprehensive exams passed, but my thesis was not yet completed. It would take five more years and as many moves to finish that final piece. I also hated to leave the community we had begun to gather in Fairbanks.

When we arrived in Georgia, my autumn friend Ann was there for the year-long assignment both our husbands had received. Her presence cushioned the pain I was feeling, and we did some things together, but I turned inward and began a serious exploration of my faith that year. Now I realize that I did not know how to share my feelings, so I retreated from our friendship and turned inward instead of talking much.

In the middle of that year in Georgia, our husbands both received orders to go to Vietnam. Ann and I plunged deeper into a winter season of silence, chilled by apprehension about the future. When the year in Georgia ended and our husbands prepared to leave for Vietnam, Ann and I agreed to call each other once a month, just to stay in touch during the lonely year ahead. The promise of sharing my fears and hopes with a friend who would be enduring a winter season like mine sustained me as I moved away from the supportive community of other "waiting wives."

**Journal Questions
Winter: Season of "Me"**

- Remember the first time you left a community that was important to you. Where did you go and why? What resources sustained you?

- Describe a winter friend. What qualities of friendship are important to you during this season?

The Circle of Seasons

- Stop for a few minutes right now and draw a circle. Label winter, spring, summer, and fall, as in the diagram.

- For each season, add the names of each friend you have identified through the journaling questions from this chapter.

- Take some time to write your own description for each season of friendship, based on your experience.

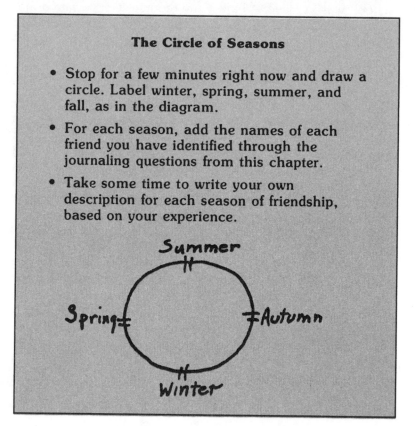

2. Winter Friendship:
   Finding My Self

Widows walking
grouped in grief
servants of custom
rather than friends. . .

Naomi stopped and said,
"Go back!
Return to your mother's house!"

One did.
Orpah ("turning away")
went back
trying to reverse the sun,
become a bride again.

One didn't.
Ruth ("beloved")
left her mother's house in Moab
for Naomi's way.
Could she leave because she was loved?

Paired by Ruth's choice
they walked
together
toward
. . . rumors of food and a future.

Naomi: Choosing Independence

When we face choices that will upset relationship patterns which sustain us, we need friends outside the system to companion us on the way. A crisis can open the psyche and also open our patterns of relationship to someone who will have a new vision of "how it could be" and is reliable enough to walk with us into that new reality. A winter friend may be an old friend who is also undergoing major change in her life at the same time, or it may be someone entirely new, someone who shares some part of the emerging pattern. Those friends are given as a gift, undeserved and unearned: grace in winter.

For Naomi, death precipitated independence. When her sons Mahlon and Chilion died, the economic base for her family in Moab was suddenly gone. Even if her sons had owned land in Moab, there were now no male family members to defend Naomi's claim to property. And without land, the older woman and her two daughters-in-law had no economic options except begging or prostitution.

Naomi acted to claim their right to life when she decided they would make the long journey back to Bethlehem. There she had some hope for survival, even if the trip itself was extremely dangerous. Yahweh was said to have visited the Hebrews and provided them with food again, bringing an end to the long famine which had originally driven Naomi and Elimelech away. And Naomi also knew that the Hebrews allowed widows to work in the fields after gleaning, so she could at least imagine that they could find enough food to survive.

The younger women Ruth and Orpah had no choice. They belonged to Naomi by tribal custom, if not by law. No longer innocent or easily married again, they prepared to leave their homeland, families, native language, and religious customs and go with Naomi. Their journey would parallel Naomi's journey some twenty years earlier: leaving home because of drought, famine, and death. But unlike Naomi's original journey to Moab, there was no male to protect them on the road and no promise of children to give them a future.

Three women in mourning set out together, but then Naomi turned to the two younger women and directed them to leave her: "Go, return each of you to her mother's house" (1:8 RSV). Her words stopped the simple flow of the story, turning custom back on itself. Although Naomi felt abandoned and unblessed, she asserted her religious authority when she voiced the hope that the God of her faith would honor the commitment of her daughters-in-law to marriage and family by providing them with another chance to have those relationships: "May the Lord deal kindly with you, as you have dealt with the dead and with me," she added (1:8 RSV).

Naomi took hold of her power to bind and to release Orpah and Ruth, speaking from the position of authority as matriarch, now the spiritual head of the family. She extended her spiritual authority and gave them God's blessing in response to their faithful service in her home. Somewhere inside herself, Naomi had discovered her grounding in God's spirit. Stripped of external security, Naomi had found a source of life that went beyond the conventional understanding of God's Law. In the eyes of some Hebrews, she and her family had been disobedient by leaving the land that was promised by God. Still, she dared to call down God's blessing on her daughters-in-law because they, as foreign women, had been kind! She was coming home to a deeper faith in this winter season.

As Naomi claimed the freedom to let Ruth and Orpah go back to their own mothers, she, too, stood at a turning-point, empty and yet determined. Naomi chose into the wintry season of being alone with her grief. She was ready to leave her role as wife and mother forever. When she directed Orpah and Ruth to return to their homeland, she was making a statement of her own independence: she was no longer willing to be the surrogate mother for them. She let go of their kindness, their dutiful support, and whatever form of friendship they had provided for her.

Seasoned by tragedy and enlivened by her own stubborn faith, Naomi was ready to walk the dangerous road toward Bethlehem by herself. Her decision marked the transition from identifying herself as a mother, to being an independent person without family ties. She no longer identified herself with the child-bearing capacity she once had. With sardonic humor she said to the younger women, "Even if I thought there was still hope for me—even if I had a husband tonight and then gave birth to sons—would you wait until they grew up? Would you remain unmarried for them?" (1:12-13).

Outwardly, Naomi confronted each of the younger women with a choice. Inwardly, she must have been wrestling with her own questions in silence as they walked. Surely she must have felt the weight of custom and responsibility for Ruth and Naomi. As she made her decision to send them back to Moab, Naomi let go of whatever identity she may have felt in their dependence on her. She chose to focus on her *self* and her own needs; she was acting as a winter friend to herself!

As women, we are encouraged from birth to think first of our relationships to others and not to stand alone. We do not grow up with the expectation that we will have to be economically or socially or spiritually self-sufficient. Like Naomi, we live in an economic and social system which encourages dependence for women. Yet most women will indeed spend a significant portion of adult life alone—by choice, widowhood, or divorce. When suddenly released from conventional relationship structures, we may experience independence as a burden rather than an opportunity. In the face of winter, we may first need to discover the inner resources that Naomi found to walk alone in the world.

In one sense, winter always requires that we choose independence. Because it is the season of death, of endings, of stillness and blankness, of solitude, we must confront our own limitations and let go of the wish-dreams that keep us bound to the past. Just as Naomi confronted the end of her sexual capacity to bear children and acknowledged that she did not see any further usefulness in her body, she still wanted to live. From her inner resources, Naomi was able to move beyond the cultural definition of meaning for a woman's life to find a new level of purpose: she acted as if Yahweh's provision of food for the Hebrews was also meant for her.

Looking back at my own life, I realize that I watch for Naomi-women now. I notice women with grey hair and hard-earned wrinkles who are living full and interesting lives alone. Virginia is one of those women. During the years that she nursed her dying husband, she built furniture and redecorated her house—doing all the work herself. During that time, she talked of color, texture, and practical problems of construction. Once her husband was gone and her daughters married, Virginia began to travel to Asia whenever she could afford it. Between trips she learned more about where she was going by immersing herself in the culture: food, friends, music, language courses, and books. Neither sentimental nor romantic about the people of Asia, she had enormous respect for the ways in which other people build a coherent life. Her stories and pictures included the practical arts of clothing and furniture, the diverse ways of earning money, the details of family life, and the scope of religious rituals. The richness of her learning will be left when she cannot go herself. Virginia's lively independence has given me a model for how to be a friend to myself and has made growing older attractive for me.

Finding My Self

- Draw a timeline of your life, in any shape that you want, indicating the ups and downs.
- Mark the major events in your life with a symbol and a date.

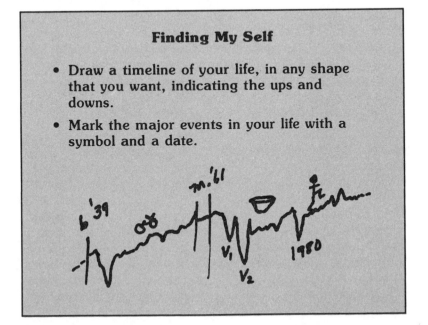

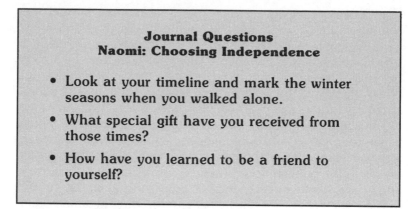

Journal Questions
Naomi: Choosing Independence

- Look at your timeline and mark the winter seasons when you walked alone.

- What special gift have you received from those times?

- How have you learned to be a friend to yourself?

Orpah: Choosing Dependence

When confronted with the choice to go back to their mothers' homes, both Orpah and Ruth initially protested and stated their intention to continue the journey with Naomi. Without any training or experience in making independent decisions for themselves, the choice must have been terrifying for them. Naomi was not only releasing them, but she was abdicating her role as caretaker and decision-maker. Unexpectedly, Ruth and Orpah were faced with making life-changing decisions for themselves. Neither had been prepared for that kind of decision-making by the culture in which they lived.

Finally, Orpah kissed her mother-in-law and turned away, returning to her own mother in Moab. The young widow went back toward girlhood, not ready to leave the protection of home and family. Although her prospects for finding a husband were not very good—since she had been married to a foreigner and produced no children—she wanted to believe in her past more than she dared to believe in Naomi's future. Her marriage had been an extension of her own mother's nurture and guidance, and Orpah made a clear choice to look for more of the same by seeking a husband among the known patterns of her past. She wanted to be a wife more than she wanted to claim her independent power as a woman, so she returned to her mother's house.

On the surface, Orpah's choice was logical. She continued to be a dutiful daughter-in-law by obeying Naomi. For her, the journey around the Dead Sea toward Bethlehem meant death because it meant giving up the dream of having a husband and children. Naomi was quite clear about the limitations which the return to Bethlehem would impose on Ruth and Orpah: Naomi could not provide the young women with husbands from Elimelech's family. And Orpah did not have the inner resources to choose the risk of an unknown path.

Like Orpah, many women try to avoid the independence that comes with the unexpected death of a spouse or with another major relational shift. Particularly if we have grown up with the dual expectation that marriage is essential for happiness, and childbearing is critical to female fulfillment, we are likely to meet the prospect of living alone with retreat, seeking refuge within the shelter of a biological family or a similar protective social grouping, like a church. There we wait for "the right man" as Orpah wanted to do.

However, Orpah's choice feels sad to me. She was not yet ready for the challenge of separating from the protective surrounding of a parental figure. When Orpah made the choice to return to her mother's house, she disappeared from the biblical story. She lost her chance to participate in the larger drama of God's presence within human history.

I made Orpah's choice when I was twenty-six and had been married five years. Peter got orders to go to Vietnam for the first time, and I had to decide where to live and what to do. At first, I thought that I would continue my college dreams of working in Washington, D.C., as a part of some political or legal office. But then, when I imagined what might happen inside of me if Peter were killed, I decided to return "to my mother's house." I called my parents in Bellingham, Washington, and asked them to find me an apartment near their home so I could be in a supportive environment. Like Orpah, I wanted to get away from the pain of winter. I returned to the community of my childhood to wait for Peter to come back. My ambition and self-confidence had eroded during the years of early marriage, and I was too frightened to walk alone. Although Peter and I were physically apart, we were emotionally bonded, and I was not free to choose for my *self* yet.

When I went back to Bellingham, I did discover new resources in an old community. Two winter friends, Jean and Louie Mideke, offered me a place in which to work with clay and a potter's wheel. Every night after I was finished teaching at the junior high, I went to Louie's studio where I worked alone. His own searching spirit was everywhere: in the hand-made tools, careful records of glazes and firings, and his day's work on the shelves. At first, I was a harsh judge of my beginning efforts. Then gradually, I learned to love the work itself: the feel of the clay, the rhythm of the wheel, the craft of making pots that sang after firing. My winter became a time to focus on my *self* and my own needs, a time for solitude and discovering internal resources.

Journal Questions
Oprah: Choosing Dependence

- Go back to the timeline that you drew in the first part of this chapter. Can you locate (or add) a turning-point when you made a choice for the familiar patterns of the past? How old were you? What were the circumstances?

- How did you make your choice?

- Where did you go? Who were your friends there? What did you learn about yourself?

Ruth: Choosing Interdependence

Ruth listened to Naomi, who urged her to follow her Moabite sister-in-law, but Ruth did not obey like a dutiful daughter. Instead, Ruth took charge of her own life by making a unilateral commitment to Naomi:

> "Wherever you go, I will go,
> wherever you live, I will live.

Your people shall be my people,
and your God, my God.
Wherever you die, I will die
and there I will be buried.
May Yahweh do this thing to me
and more also,
if even death should come between us!" (1:16-17 JB)

Ruth's shocking statement was an act of total commitment to the death and beyond. With these words, Ruth let go of everything that had sustained her in the past. Out of her own wintry place of death and mysterious inner hope for life, Ruth chose into a future with Naomi that was based in Naomi's faith tradition. Ruth's pledge moved their relationship from the known roles of an extended family into the unknown risks of being on a dangerous journey together.

Somehow Ruth was ready to leave her mother's house. She was ready to move on from the dependent roles of daughter and wife to the independent stance of being a separate woman. The meaning of her name may give us a clue: she was "beloved." Maybe some special affection or attention had given her the courage to step into an adult relationship with Naomi. Whatever the reason, rather than return to the patterns of the past, Ruth claimed the power to risk a barren future with no guarantees.

Ruth not only left her own mother's house, but she released Naomi from the responsibility of mothering as well. Instead of bargaining with Naomi or asking her to continue her role as the mother-in-law and protector, Ruth simply asked Naomi not to command her to leave. Ruth was ready to be her own woman and, because of that, she was also ready for a different kind of relationship with Naomi. They could be friends.

With her decision to accompany Naomi, Ruth moved from a shadowy role in Naomi's life, as an "appendage" of Mahlon, toward a more equal partnership. Ruth shifted their friendship from winter aloneness toward springtime nurturing, but Naomi was silent in response. While she did not refuse Ruth's commitment, Naomi did not welcome it either. Naomi stayed in her wintry mode while they trudged toward Bethlehem together.

Literally, Ruth was ready for the dangerous journey ahead: politically, they had no system to cover them; physically, they were no match for armed men. They would have to walk in faith, willing to die if necessary. But psychologically, Ruth had reached the point in her life where such a risk did not matter to her. The choice to love Naomi and walk with her toward an unknown future was a choice for life, for unlimited possibility.

Figuratively, the scope of Ruth's commitment was larger than the immediate issue of accompanying Naomi on a dangerous journey. Ruth chose into God's story unilaterally. Her pledge took her beyond Naomi to the history and belief system of another people. During her ten years within Naomi's Hebrew family, Ruth would have heard stories of the covenant, the Exodus journey, and the commandments of Yahweh, along with the many guidelines for community life which were passed on aurally. She would have experienced the power and mystery of Naomi's faith in Yahweh, which was strong enough to call the older woman back to Bethlehem after all the years in Moab. When the choice came, Ruth was ready to respond. She committed herself to Naomi, and the older woman's faith was large enough to guide them both.

We don't know why Ruth was ready to make this choice while Orpah was not. Perhaps Ruth had no family, or perhaps it was too violent or too crowded for her to find a place with them in Moab. Maybe she had more capacity for vision or faith. We must remember that both Ruth and Orpah had shared Naomi's household for a decade prior to the commitment that Ruth made. The difference between them was in Ruth's readiness for interdependence. Whatever the reason, Ruth was ready to leave her biological background, her people and their gods, and choose into the religious context of Naomi's life.

When Ruth closed her pledge with the words, "May Yahweh do this thing to me and more," she made Naomi's God the authority behind her own promise. Ruth came to the covenant "by faith." She knew what to do and how to do it intuitively. According to Jewish law, her action would have been called "circumcision of the heart" (Deuteronomy 10:16). Her pledge was the outward sign of an inward change that had already occurred.

There is no indication that Ruth felt chosen by God or by Naomi. Instead, Ruth made her own commitment as a responsible female adult, with no male intercessor. The words of Ruth's pledge were the words of an adult woman who had left the innocent belief that having a husband would complete her life. Seared by her losses and disappointments, Ruth made her pledge to Naomi in a way that marked the beginning of a lifetime friendship that would span many seasons and differences between them, a friendship that would become the vehicle of God's presence in the story.

To see Ruth's commitment to Naomi as a pledge of friendship may be a surprise to contemporary readers. We usually hear Ruth's pledge in a traditional marriage ceremony: ". . . until death do us part." Those words were read as Peter and I turned from the altar toward the doors of the church at the end of our wedding service. Of all the biblical promises for commitment in relationship, Ruth's pledge seemed most appropriate for our marriage. To me, it was the best biblical model for the kind of friendship that I hoped to develop with Peter. At the time, the cost of making such a commitment did not seem too high: I wanted to leave my land and people for his; his God seemed to be the same as mine; and I believed that marriage did mean "until death do us part." At that time, I did not understand the interdependence of the pledge, but I hoped that something good would be born of my total commitment.

On the surface level, Ruth's pledge may seem like yet another form of dependence: I'll do what you do. But the inner dimension of the commitment signaled Ruth's ability to take hold of the decision-making power: she was ready to take responsibility for her own decisions, to set her own priorities, and to commit her time and energy. As we reach the level of freedom that Ruth had reached, through the trials and disappointments of our own lives, we too can decide our futures. We can take the risk of moving beyond the cultural conventions that require women to depend on parents or a husband for personal identity; we can choose when, where, how, and to whom we will commit ourselves.

When Peter got orders to go to Vietnam a second time, I was able to make Ruth's choice instead of Orpah's. I was ready to let go of Peter. Instead of returning "to my mother's house," I chose to stay at Dartmouth College in New Hampshire where I was the women's counselor.

Part of the reason I was ready to choose a more independent path was my friend Joanne. We had been part of the same church congregation in Hanover, New Hampshire, but had never spoken about things that mattered deeply until we happened to room together at a church retreat. The intense and structured retreat environment gave us an opportunity to discover the thinking/wondering/searching selves behind roles that had kept us apart, polite and distant. After Peter was sent to Vietnam, Joanne made a commitment to "be family" for me: she included me for dinner twice a week, and she was willing to walk in the darker places of my fears when I was willing to talk. I often sat with Joanne and her family in church, where the rituals and prayers gave me space to grieve for lost dreams and face the reality of my life without Peter's companionship.

I learned something about interdependence that year. Joanne made it clear that we each brought something different to our friendship. As a mother with two young daughters, she offered me a home and family. As a college faculty member, I offered her conversation and ideas in areas that were not being encouraged in her role as a mother. And we both shared a lively interest in theology. Our reciprocal contributions to the friendship made my winter journey a time of self-discovery rather than self-pity.

Journal Questions
Ruth: Choosing Interdependence

- Give an example of a time in your life when you felt dependent. Then, give an example of a time when you shared interdependence with someone. What or who enabled you to make the freer choice?

- Have you ever made a commitment "until death," either to yourself or to another person?

- If so, what does that commitment mean to you now?

Ruth and Naomi: Sharing Independence

Winter friendships require a certain level of independence for the commitment that is necessary to weather this season of solitude. The nurturing aspect of spring is missing; the stimulation of summer seems far away; and the comfortable camaraderie of autumn is replaced by the painful need for each one to take care of herself and simply be present to the other. At times, one friend may break through the shell of silence with tenderness more than demand: like porcupines, winter friends "make love" carefully, often at a distance from one another.

The winter friendship of Ruth and Naomi began in silence as they walked together toward Bethlehem. Like time-lapse photography, the writer simply reports that "the two women went on until they came to Bethlehem" (1:19). But human relationships take place in time and space, and Ruth's commitment must have been tested a hundred times on that long trip. Naomi's willingness to have Ruth with her must have been tested as well.

Naomi had already asserted her independence: she had been prepared to make the journey by herself, to die on the road if necessary. In obedience to her inner guidance and rumors of God's favor to her own people, Naomi reclaimed her faith in the covenant promise, "I will take you as my own people, and I will be your God (Exodus 6:7 NIV). Without other family responsibilities for the first time in her life, she was free to respond without considering the needs of others. She was, at last, ready for her own spiritual journey.

But the reality of Ruth's companionship, confirmed by the strength of Ruth's independent commitment, required a partnership on the trip that Naomi had not invited. Naomi and Ruth were now linked together in their hazardous journey toward Bethlehem. As winter friends, they could endure hardship and survive challenge because they were basically independent of each other. They had each made their decision and were ready to move on. They did not feed each other directly; their interaction was oblique. They walked beside each other, committed to the relationship and yet alone, reflective, and aware of how vulnerable they were to the threat of death.

The shadow of death links winter friends to the ultimate mysteries of life and love, transcending the boundaries of language. The deep and often unspoken spiritual connections between winter friends grow out of primitive or preverbal experiences. The bonding between winter friends carries both the fear and the promise of experience that goes beyond rational calculation. Making a commitment to live with another against the backdrop of death makes a winter friendship qualitatively different from those of other seasons where the interaction is more visible, more common, and more friendly.

Like Ruth and Naomi on their desert journey, winter friends draw from the same deep spiritual well, but they are likely to offer each other different gifts on the surface. They feed on their own inner resources, while adjusting their actions enough to cooperate. In some ways winter friends share the dark side of life because they are individually acquainted with grief and loss. I suspect that aging is also a factor for most people: at midlife, the reality of death may become more conscious and may color most of our important relationships with this season of friendship.

My own winter friends are those who are able to share some sense of what I am going through without a lot of explanation. They may not have experienced exactly the same thing, but their lives have been touched by pain in some way that opens us to each other without many words. Sometimes I do not know myself that I have passed into a winter season, so it takes the pain of another to touch my silent self and draw me into relationship. But when the winter season in my life is more obvious, like the times when I am moving from one place to another, then I watch for a soul-mate who will not be too demanding or who can receive my listening and my grieving until I can begin to establish a sense of being at home and alive. Until that happens, I feel invisible.

After Peter returned from his second tour in Vietnam, we moved to Springfield, Virginia. As with each prior move, I experienced the bleak landscape of winter in my soul, but this time I gave myself to the inward journey of Naomi. I knew what to do in a winter season in order to reach the inner source that I now recognize as God's spirit: I borrowed the money to set up my own commercial pottery studio in the basement of our townhouse. Slowly the clay provided a tangible process for healing the wound of displacement. The work itself provided a simple rhythm for releasing my anger and experiencing the joy of creativity. I let go of my self-image as a college faculty member and explored the discipline of my craft.

Soon after I began to sell my pots, I met Lois through a mutual friend. She asked if I would teach her to work with clay, but I refused, saying "When I teach, I don't produce . . . and it's important for me to make pots right now." Like Ruth, Lois didn't take my answer as her only choice. Instead she asked to come and sit quietly in my studio, "to watch and learn," she said. With three sons under the age of five, Lois told me that she needed an hour of quiet with another adult each week. I could agree to that, so she came and sat with me. Although Lois and I did not face a physical life-and-death situation, we each needed the other to companion our way into feeling alive in spirit again. We enjoyed our silence together, and she did not move into more discussion until I was ready. Like Ruth, her commitment was one-sided. Like Naomi, the direction of our friendship was set by my needs, but somehow our shared presence was enough for both our wintry souls.

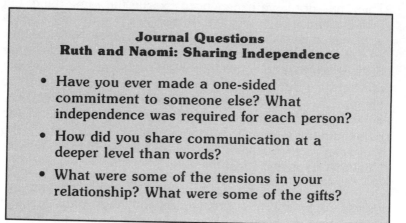

Journal Questions
Ruth and Naomi: Sharing Independence

- Have you ever made a one-sided commitment to someone else? What independence was required for each person?

- How did you share communication at a deeper level than words?

- What were some of the tensions in your relationship? What were some of the gifts?

3. Spring Friendship:
Being New Together

Bitter, but real,
    Naomi was welcomed
        by Bethlehem.
Invisible, unnamed,
    Ruth was ignored
        as a foreigner.

They couldn't live without eating
    so Ruth went to work
        in the fields
    where God
gave them food for life.

From silence to speech
    the women claimed "we"
        as they mothered each other—
    aware in their words
of God's sheltering wings.

Safety

Spring friendship, the season of "we," develops as two people learn to trust each other for basic needs: safety, nurture, and speech. Finding a safe place to begin a new phase or test a new level of trust is not easy for adults. We live in a culture that puts a premium on confidence and control. When newborn parts of our lives are shared with someone else, we may experience fear at the childlike vulnerability thus exposed. When a partner responds with care and concern for the infant beginnings that continue to occur all through adult life, then a spring friendship is born.

When Ruth and Naomi finally arrived in Bethlehem, their external journey together had ended safely, but their internal journey together was still just beginning. They were delivered from a mysteriously protected womb-life together in the wilderness to a physical struggle for survival in Naomi's homeland, without any man to give them a legitimate place there.

The appearance of the two women after their long dangerous journey caused the villagers to gather around with a buzz of excitement. Like birds on a warm spring morning, the women of Bethlehem chattered and exclaimed about Naomi's return, wanting to know about her life since she had left. Ruth was completely ignored in all the commotion.

For her part, Naomi refused the crowd's rejoicing and named herself Mara, "because the Almighty has made my life very bitter," she said (1:20). Although she and Elimelech had departed from Bethlehem because of famine, she remembered having left "full" with a husband and two sons, and now she was returning "empty" because they were gone. In her own mind Naomi had left at the peak of her womanly power, even though the land was barren. Now the land was full, and she was the barren one, the hollow vessel. Naomi kept her wintry stance as she entered the village. Something—or someone—was needed to connect her with the food and community joyfulness in Bethlehem. By declaring that she had come back without family, Naomi denied Ruth's very presence. The older woman had no language to express whatever hope she may have felt in her relationship with Ruth.

The people of Bethlehem did not see that the two women from Moab could give birth to anything new either. Their interaction with Naomi seemed to focus on childbearing, which excluded Ruth entirely. Having left her own mother's house and land, Ruth initially found no place among the women of Naomi's homeland, nor did she receive any help from Naomi. The springtime relationships which Bethlehem valued were heterosexual pairs and mothers with children, not the chosen friendship of two widows. Ruth might as well have been invisible.

Although the covenant faith of the Israelites decreed welcome to the stranger and sojourner, Naomi and Ruth challenged the conventional patterns of relationship by arriving together with no place to go, no family or clan to provide a home for them. Naomi was welcomed with excitement because she was known and remembered. She already had roots in the community stemming from her marriage to Elimelech, but her participation would have to take a new form because she had been gone so long and was now in a very different relationship from her original Bethlehem-blessed marriage. Not only would Naomi and Ruth have to find a form for their friendship within the traditional patterns of marriage and family, but the community would have to change because of their arrival. Ultimately, that would mean finding a new way of understanding how God's provision extended to a foreigner. But, in the beginning, Bethlehem offered Naomi and Ruth a place to be together and nothing else.

Whatever bonding had taken place between the older woman and the younger one while they traveled in the desert remained unspoken. They had not yet become a pair, a clearly defined "we" of spring friends. The village women could not name them as partners either, because the Bethlehem language was limited to thinking in conventional dyads: married couples, mothers with children, and auxiliary family groupings. Since Ruth could not participate in this community through her own children, she remained an outsider. And from Naomi's reaction, describing herself as "bitter," we know that she, too, saw her value in this particular community solely on the basis of a mother's role, no matter how rich her living experiences had been. Both women were aliens to the cultural norms for women in Bethlehem.

Thus, although their arrival in Bethlehem signaled a shift in the external season of their friendship from winter into spring, conditions were chilly and unpredictable. Naomi's bitterness matched Ruth's marginal status, and the two women bonded in their need. As the spring season of their friendship began to develop within the social context of Bethlehem, Naomi seemed helpless as a child. She did not seek assistance from anyone of Elimelech's clan. Instead, she was like a newborn, just arrived in Bethlehem and totally dependent. If they were going to survive, Ruth needed to take on the mothering role and find some way to provide food and shelter for both of them, but neither one could provide physical safety for Ruth if she left the village to work in the fields. In the beginning they settled for trusting each other within a hostile environment.

Finding a place where spring friendship can develop with some safety and protection is not easy for women today either. Women are socialized to create a home for others and to identify with the mothering role so thoroughly that there is no time or space for being a child in those relationships. For many women, the family is a closed circle and female friendships must take place around the edges. Women who have learned to make time and space for female friendships will recognize the importance of spring friendships in giving birth to new stages in adult life. Going beyond the cultural definitions of a mothering role means finding space to enter the frightening vulnerability of a child-mother pattern once again. Many women do that with a therapist. Others discover a spring friend with whom they can share the journey.

In the beginning the commitment to a spring friendship may be one-sided, as Ruth's was, but the direction will be set by the other's need, like Naomi's. That imbalance exists at the heart of a mother-child dyad, and it may be repeated in adulthood whenever one person experiences a crisis of new growth and another responds with care or concern. Initially, this connection may carry overtones of our earliest bonded relationship between mother and child. But the basic dyad is repeated in female friendships with a vital difference: neither partner is locked into one role or the other. We shift back and forth between the child and mother roles, providing safety and companionship for each other through some new stage of life. In that process, spring friends draw boundaries around their "we-ness" and define a way of being together that gives spring friends a unique identity as a pair.

In my own life, I found the beginning of the safety of spring friendship in my pottery studio. As I was creating my niche in the marketplace of northern Virginia crafts, my winter friend Lois continued to visit my studio regularly. I began to relax my intense drive to produce and to look forward to her visits. I found I could share the excitement of my new discoveries in form and technique, as well as my doubts about being an artist and the disappointments of costly mistakes as I worked on glaze experiments. With her sustained commitment to be *with* me, she provided enough safety for me to be vulnerable as a beginner.

Eventually Lois also began to work with clay by hand instead of learning to use the wheel. In my basement studio she found a safe place to develop a new skill, and she gave me a chance to remember the part of myself that loved to teach. We offered each other a place to learn new skills and to reflect on our lives beyond marriage and family. Like Ruth and Naomi, we learned to trust our time together; our process of reciprocal mother-child nurturing created the safety in which our spring friendship grew.

**Journal Questions
Safety**

- What qualities or conditions make you feel safe enough to risk a new beginning in friendship?
- Have you ever experienced an external threat or challenge that promoted internal bonding in a spring friendship? How did you and your friend create safety for each other?

Nurture

Just as a baby requires food for life and growth, a spring friendship requires care and feeding. The biological role that women play in suckling children has been extended by our culture into nurturing the entire family—physically, emotionally, and spiritually. Women are often depleted by that role and must learn to recognize how they have denied their own needs for the sake of others. A female friendship, where neither partner is locked into being the nurturing mother or the needy child, may be a vital necessity for restoring the balance of give and take in one's life. Nurturing between women takes many forms, but it begins with the question, "What do you need?," followed by, "How can I provide that for you?"

Ruth initiated the next part of the story: she went to work in the fields to provide food for herself and Naomi. Bereft of a male provider and protector, she broke the conventions of age and dependency and acted to support herself and Naomi. "Let me go to the fields," she told Naomi, "and pick up the leftover grain" (2:2). Although couched as a request, Ruth's intention was clear: she was ready to take whatever risks were necessary to insure their survival.

Hebrew law directed landowners not to reap their fields to the border or clean the fields after harvest, so that the poor could find enough food to sustain life (Leviticus 19:10). Although Ruth knew that the men in the fields preyed on the unprotected, she hoped to "find favor" from someone who would be kind to her. Because she had already crossed the boundary of staying safe at home when she left Moab, she could choose to leave the safety of Bethlehem's streets and go out into the grain fields. She had already confronted her fears of physical violation and starvation when she committed herself to a relationship with Naomi (and with Naomi's God). Through a combination of trust and desperation, Ruth was ready to take her pledge to Naomi one step further and enter the harvest fields to find food, risking attack or violation for the sake of life itself.

Ruth's courage stirred Naomi out of wintry silence: "Go ahead, my daughter," she said (2:2), claiming a family tie that honored Ruth's commitment. Naomi had long since let go of her mother-in-law role when they stood on the desert road and watched Orpah leave, but now she moved into a new level of relationship with Ruth. Naomi's use of the word "daughter" moved her back into a mothering role, proclaimed her willingness to make Ruth part of her family, and signified her readiness to link Ruth with the community into which the younger woman had already chosen. Naomi named their kinship as an intentional family, freely chosen by each of them. Her blessing was the first sign of *mutual* commitment to their friendship.

The older woman had come back to Bethlehem because "she heard in Moab that the Lord had come to the aid of his people by providing food for them" (1:6). And even if Naomi could not join Ruth in the fields to help gather grain or provide some protection for her, she could claim a more active role in linking Ruth to the community. The biblical narrator provides a clue to that connection by prefacing Ruth's decision to work in the fields with the fact that "Naomi had a relative on her husband's side, from the clan of Elimelech, a man of standing, whose name was Boaz (2:1). Thus Naomi carried the thread of clan connection for both of them, while Ruth's determination to work provided the link between Naomi's unclaimed family ties and their future together.

Naomi's response moved their friendship solidly into spring where it could flower and hope to bear fruit. Although their "mutual mothering" was limited at first, they blessed each other and shared hope for the future because Ruth dared to act. Together they affirmed that there was life for women beyond marriage and motherhood, even in their patriarchal society.

In our own day, spring friendships function in much the same way: as a primary pairing from which the energy for taking risks can come. Often a marriage or an old friendship can function as a basic unit of trust, but the encouragement for an emerging aspect of self will come from a friendship where growth can extend beyond usual patterns. We often discover nurturing partners at a new place of work or through a new activity which gives objective form to a new stage of development. Those partners can nourish the new growth because they are not invested in maintaining earlier life patterns.

When entering a new and/or hostile environment, we all need somebody who will say "Go ahead, my daughter." The tone in which the words are said makes all the difference. A mother still struggling with the fusion of childhood might, after a long argument, grudgingly say to a teenage daughter, "Go ahead." But a friend who stands in that mothering role can freely bless a new endeavor without needing to control the outcome. As a commitment to care about what happens, the words "Go ahead, my daughter" characterize spring friendships that encourage growth and risk. The blessing and encouragement of those words literally feed one's emerging self.

A slightly older friend who gave me the encouragement to "go ahead" was my neighbor in Springfield, Virginia. Dawn was a serious painter and a gourmet cook, taking courses in graduate school toward a degree in fine arts. I was a little bit awed by her attention because she seemed so complete and so independent. She loved the plates and cups and bowls I was making in my pottery studio and used them frequently. She was knowledgeable about different galleries where I might enter shows, and she urged me to take samples of my work where I would have been afraid to go. Like Naomi, Dawn could not do the work for me, but she was aware of the difficulties and she helped me to be realistic about my chances for success in different marketplaces.

As our friendship deepened, she spoke of the more vulnerable parts of her life, and there were times when I played the mothering role in our spring friendship. Listening to her talk, reflecting back what I had heard, and holding her pain gently between us, I gave Dawn a place to explore new growth in some of her other relationships. We nurtured each other with good food, frank talk and energetic, if not skillful, tennis. At the core of our spring friendship was an agreement to care about what was happening for the other.

Journal Questions
Nurture

- How do you nurture a special friendship?
- Consider the ways in which you are "fed" by a spring friend.

Dialogue

If safety and nurture are two important aspects of a spring friendship, then a third vital aspect is dialogue: developing a language of love so the relationship can thrive over time and in memory. Dialogue between friends is an important way of describing something *new* that is taking place. Bringing images to speech provides a way of interpreting and understanding what is coming into being. The combination of safety, nurture, and speech give us a sense of belonging, of being "at home" in the world. As a mother helps a child develop speech as a tool for moving away from her, dialogue with a spring friend helps us move on toward summer.

Ruth's decision to enter the ripened fields of Bethlehem allowed her to participate directly in the abundance that Yahweh had provided for the Hebrews. Her actions placed the interdependent bond between her and Naomi within the context of God's care and protection. Her work affirmed her choice to leave the barren land and the death of her marriage in Moab.

As a field hand in Bethlehem, she would share in the physical and spiritual bounty of God's provision.

When Ruth entered the grain fields, she hoped for someone who would look on her with favor. "As it turned out," the biblical narrator states, "[Ruth] found herself working in a field belonging to Boaz" (2:3). Ruth was already under the protective wing of Yahweh, but she had to live out her part of the dramatic story in order for God's provision to be seen. She was the catalyst for God's active care, not just the recipient.

When Boaz came to his field and noticed Ruth, he asked his foreman, "Whose young woman is that?" (2:5). The foreman described Ruth by the characteristic that was important to the people of Bethlehem: her identity as a foreigner who had come back with Naomi. He also made note of her hard-working dedication, saying, "[She] has worked steadily from morning till now, except for a short rest in the shelter" (2:8). It became clear to Boaz that Ruth belonged to Naomi by her own commitment. Even in the field, her mother-daughter relationship was acknowledged. As the discussion moved away from male ownership to Ruth's qualities as an independent person, the two men provided language to describe the cultural shift that would eventually include Ruth among the people of Bethlehem.

Boaz was surprised to learn that Ruth belonged to no man. He was quick to offer her the protection she lacked, saying that she should stay with his crew of gleaning women, that he had directed the men "not to touch you," and further, that she could drink from the water they had drawn (2:9). Like a good father, he gave her the safety and nurture in a public arena that Ruth's friendship with Naomi provided in the personal and private sphere.

Ruth's independence, courage, and lively curiosity were shown by her question to Boaz: "Why have I found such favor in your eyes that you notice me—a foreigner?" (2:10). She did not attribute the favor to God, but met Boaz face-to-face with her question. Her tone was direct, her self-confidence probably surprising to Boaz. She named her role as an outsider and forced him to verbalize his relationship to her. This was no coy flirtation, but it was the beginning of a dialogue which would provide language for her place in Bethlehem. Ruth asked a probing question that pushed beyond the boundaries of propriety and humble acceptance of Boaz' beneficence. She was no child of his, nor was she a humble servant or piece of property.

Boaz answered in terms of her sacrifice for Naomi, saying that Ruth's willingness to leave her homeland and come with Naomi had touched him. He also extended the discussion beyond his own response to Ruth to the outer limits of his system of thought: "May the Lord repay you for what you have done. May you be richly rewarded by the Lord, the God of Israel, under whose wings you have come to take refuge" (2:12). His words gave Ruth an image for what was already happening: the God of Israel was like a bird providing protection for her chicks. Thus Boaz expanded their dialogue from the immediate, literal question of Ruth's safety and nourishment to the world of spirit, of covenant promise, and God's presence around them.

On the surface, Boaz' words tell us a good deal about him. He admired Ruth's commitment to Naomi. He was sensitive to what it meant to be a foreigner among the Hebrews. He was aware of Ruth's vulnerability in a strange land. According to the New Testament genealogy of Jesus, Boaz had a foreign mother himself: Rahab, the harlot in Jericho who saved Gideon and his men (Matthew 1:6). Because his mother had been a foreigner who would have been slaughtered by the invading Israelites except for her special role in helping to protect them, Boaz understood Ruth's need for protection. As Rahab's descendent, he was now in a position to offer protection to another woman as Ruth acted with courage and determination to find refuge under God's wings.

After assuring Ruth of his protection, Boaz invited her to share food as well: "She ate all she wanted and had some left over" (2:14). Ruth took the excess home to Naomi, who recognized the sign of God's provision for both of them. "The Lord has not stopped showing his kindness to the living and the dead," Naomi said, acknowledging Boaz' family ties with Elimelech (2:20). Naomi must have remembered the rumor that God had provided food for her people and recognized the generosity of Boaz as a sign to her from God.

The dialogue between Ruth and Boaz gave a new and larger context to what was happening around and through them. When Ruth asked why Boaz had paid attention to her as a foreigner, she was probing for language to describe what was already taking place. Ruth clearly felt seen, known, respected, and loved. She named the role that normally would have kept her outside of the community of Bethlehem and outside of the covenant: she was a foreigner. She asked Boaz to articulate the connection from his position inside the community norms which would have rejected her. He replied, "I've been told all about what you have done...how you left your father and mother and your homeland and came to live with a people you did not know before" (2:11). Boaz saw her from a larger perspective, with God's eyes, instead of within the limitations of his own culture. Their dialogue revealed his feeling for Ruth and his hope that God would reveal a way to include Ruth among the covenant people of Judah.

As Ruth received Boaz' care and attention, his words also interpreted Ruth's actions from the standpoint of his own covenant faith, helping Ruth to understand that she did have a place among the covenant people by virtue of God's provision. We, too, can help each other interpret and understand events that might seem unrelated: we can hear each other into speech and love each other into wholeness.

We all need to be seen as Ruth was, with loving eyes. When somebody notices, with tenderness and affection, who we are and what we are doing in the world, we can name the new life within us. Underneath the question "Why have you noticed me?" is the hope that we are loved by others and by God, that we have a right to be alive and to be nurtured toward further life.

Every time we are seen and named by those who love us, we are empowered to live more fully, more freely. A good mother does that from the very beginning, as her child is learning to walk and talk. When we grow up, we still need to hear those same words of blessing for the stumbling and awkward parts of our lives. If we are seen with loving eyes, as Ruth was, then sharing language becomes a process of building hope and faith in the larger human community. Finding words and images for our feelings or intuitions brings the power of understanding to our previously unnamed actions, and then we ourselves become living words to others. Spring friends engage in dialogue as Boaz did with Ruth, naming what has not been understood before.

Although most of my close friends have been women, there have been men who have shared a season of friendship. The friend who helped me find speech for the spiritual dimensions of my work as a potter was an Episcopal priest whom I met at an art show. Michael was sitting with his wife's paintings for the day and there were few customers, so we had lots of time to talk. Like Boaz, he responded openly and moved easily from particular observations to spiritual connections and images. He saw beyond the surface of my words and heard the undercurrents of my questions: he listened with his eyes. When Peter came to help me pack up my display, we went to their house and soon discovered friendship as two couples. Within the safety of that foursome, Michael and I began to nurture our relationship by sharing our inner worlds of dream images, poetry, and biblical stories, as well as the external world of meals and movies that we enjoyed as couples. Spring friendship developed as we discovered safety, nurture, and language for newborn parts of our lives.

A mutual interest in spiritual aspects of the physical world—the stories behind old tools and trunks, the mystery of shell-shapes and falling stars in the night sky—has continued to feed our friendship over the years. During a later period when we lived in different cities, writing letters helped us continue to put those images and intuitions into words. Infrequent family visits and periodic retreats which I led in Michael's church provided us with meetings in which I felt seen with caring eyes and named with gentle words—mothered by a man. The language of our spring friendship has been laced with stories from the past, both personal and cultural, with books and images from the present, and with dreams of the future. Underneath the words runs a tender quality of care and attention for the newborn parts of our lives.

Journal Questions
Dialogue

- When have you experienced dialogue with someone who cares about your new beginnings?

- How has your dialogue with this spring friend helped you see your life in a larger context?

- What are some of the ways in which you communicate beyond words—in photos, objects, clothing, songs, poetry?

4. Summer Friendship:
Searching for Call and Identity

Summer
season of I
"Is it not my duty," Naomi said,
to see you settled?"
Hungry for place and for progeny
Naomi spoke.

Ruth listened
heard call
but did not see the path.
"I will do whatever you say."
Ready...
waiting.

"Go wash and anoint yourself,"
Naomi counseled,
"then go to him by night
and he will tell you what to do."
Wise woman speaking;
Ruth did as she was told.

Then the risk was Ruth's.
She went to the threshing floor,
her body a sacrament
for them both.
Boaz lay alone with
winter in his soul.

He didn't tell her what to do,
but asked instead, "Who are you?"
"Redeem us," she asked.
"I will," he whispered,
"but stay with me til dawn..."
She did.

As light brushed the sky
she left
with food as a pledge:
full-filled.
"Now we must wait,"
Naomi said.

Hunger

In summer relationships we experience hunger and thirst for something more or something different because the sources of springtime nourishment have dried up, or simply because we are human and we grow toward independence, establishing our "I am" in the world. We reach beyond the confines of home to find new work to do in the world or, at a deeper level, to discover our "call" from God. Differences become sharper, clearer, as we separate "I" from "you," and learn to put the distance into words. Summer friends are usually individuals who travel alone, not in pairs, experiencing a surge of risk, initiative, and independence.

The summer season of friendship came to Naomi and Ruth as the barley harvest came to an end. Naomi was still hungry for a place to belong and for progeny to continue the family name in Bethlehem. She had already experienced the shift from food to famine many years before when, as a young wife, she and Elimelech had fled their starving homeland in search of food. She was even more vulnerable this time as an older woman with a younger female partner, without a male in the cultural system of Bethlehem. Naomi knew they would have to do something radical in order to survive. They had no "safety net" of family or friends, although Naomi could see possibilities for help from Boaz. Naomi's impulse to provide for herself embodied her part of God's story. In faith, nourished by Ruth's diligence and favor from Boaz, Naomi began to imagine something even bolder for the sake of their future together.

"My daughter," Naomi began, "is it not my duty to see you happily settled? And is not Boaz. . .our kinsman?" (3:1 JB). Then Naomi proposed a dangerous scheme that could have brought disgrace and possible death to them both if it had failed: she encouraged Ruth to approach Boaz at night, on the threshing floor, to ask him to exercise the right of redemption over them.

When Naomi asked rhetorically, "Is not Boaz our kinsman?", she must have known or guessed that there were nearer relatives she would have to by-pass. Earlier in the story, she had realized that Boaz was related to Elimelech and therefore could be their redeemer, although the Hebrew custom of levirate succession reserved that responsibility for immediate family, and Elimelech apparently had no brothers. Now she was ready to act on a daring plan to circumvent the claims of any nearer relative and secure a family for herself and Ruth. Naomi's hunger for a home where they could be "happily settled" was the motive behind the risky plan which she proposed to Ruth.

Ruth did not seem concerned about finding a male protector in Bethlehem or with having children. At this point in the story, she was willing to obey Naomi's intuition and to follow Naomi's directions. Differences in their ages and energy levels reinforced the cultural differences between them: Naomi knew the customs and laws of Bethlehem, while Ruth probably did not know what their options really were. Naomi was seeking a more permanent place in the community for both of them, while Ruth focused on the daily task of providing food. They each brought their separate strengths to the relationship.

Today, we still live with the tension between the long-term vision of Naomi and the immediate physical needs which Ruth met. On the surface, we live in a culture that expects women to be "happily settled": finding a husband, and thus financial security, should be enough fulfillment and identity for any woman. But most women recognize a deeper call to life that is a combination of being at home with oneself and doing something in the world, something that is an expression of "I am." One's call may be expressed through marriage, but there are many other ways for women to experience God's call to life. The search for our call to BE ALIVE emerges in the restlessness of our summer souls—probing, risking, and reaching beyond what we know and have. And when we share that hungering and thirsting with someone who is also reaching beyond her present situation, we find a summer friend to walk with for a while.

A summer season came for me when Peter and I moved to Leavenworth, Kansas, from Virginia. When we learned we would be staying for three years, we bought a Victorian house in town, joined the Presbyterian church, and I set up a teaching studio in the basement of a craft-supply store. Externally, we had a secure place in the community. Internally, I was restless and hungry for something more. When one of my pottery students offered a class on "Discovering Gifts" at the church, I took it. When she challenged me to pick up my teaching gifts and offer a class for adults, I followed her suggestion. And when she urged me to attend a Faith at Work week-long event, I went: Lura had become my Naomi in Leavenworth. I suspect she, too, wanted someone to talk with about her own summer search. Her needs fed my hunger and we became summer friends.

Journal Questions
Hunger

- Go back to the timeline that you drew in chapter two and mark any periods of restless search that took you in a new direction.

- Was there a friend who took the role of Naomi for you? Or a friend like Ruth, for whom you saw a larger picture?

- How did your hungers draw you together?

Preparation

Taking a new step involves preparation: imagining what the new situation will be like, choosing clothes that seem right, doing some activity that marks letting go of the present to embark on something new. Traditionally, we focus our energies with ritual behavior: athletes go through a specific routine before an important contest, musicians prepare for a concert in practiced ways. Most of us have special ways to focus our spiritual energies, the focused light of "I am," for a particular task. Because the preparation may require intense study or complete withdrawal, a summer friend is one who will assist, or support, or understand the need for such preparation.

In the biblical story Naomi simply told Ruth what to do: "Wash and perfume yourself, and put on your best clothes. Then go down to the threshing floor, but don't let him know you are there until he has finished eating and drinking" (3:3). Naomi took the part of a priest or wisdom figure, telling Ruth exactly how to proceed. The plan was simple and dangerous: after her preparation, Ruth would go to the threshing floor under cover of darkness, find Boaz among the other men, lie down with him until he awoke, and then follow his directions from there on.

Ruth's preparation was an important aspect of Naomi's direction. Not only was Ruth to make herself as attractive as possible, but the cleansing ritual had religious overtones as well. This was to be a sacred journey, a ritual descent into darkness and danger. She would have to pass among the very field hands who had posed a threat to her safety when she had first gone to work in the fields; she would become "fair game" for any of them who awoke to find her on the threshing floor in the darkness. Then she would have to approach the man who had power to destroy or redeem her life. Ruth had to leave the safety of her home with Naomi to undertake a classical heroic journey as she walked the path between death and redemption on her way toward Boaz.

"I will do whatever you say," Ruth answered Naomi (3:5). She became the obedient initiate, committing herself to Naomi's plan without considering any other options. She trusted Naomi's wisdom and guidance, and believed in her own readiness for the task ahead.

The ritual of washing and anointing herself was a time of preparing her body and spirit for the dangerous task. When Ruth washed her body, she was not only cleansing her skin but she may have been washing away her fears as well. When she anointed her body, she was softening her skin with oil and perfume, but the word "anointed" also carried the connotation of a holy work being set apart by the oil. Ruth's preparation was a sign of her own priestly power as she chose to risk her life for a larger goal that would unfold from the dynamics of what lay ahead.

Claiming someone else's vision for our lives, as Ruth did, involves an intentional decision which can be solidified by ritual preparation. We may dress carefully, choosing particular colors or styles that we feel enhance or extend our personal power. We may pray, to center our spirits and connect with the larger reality of God's presence. We may also add fasting and communion or other shared rituals, if a community is part of our preparation.

Although we live in a material culture where "what you see is what you get," most of us sense a spiritual reality pervading the physical, and ritual is one way of connecting with that intangible realm of spirit. In recent years women have formed ritual groups around the country to celebrate many different aspects of their lives that have been neglected by formal religious practices: changing seasons in nature, personal transitions, family and community junctures. Just as Ruth washed and anointed herself for her sacred journey to the threshing floor, we gather our powers and cleanse our souls for the trials that mark our lives. We recognize that rituals of recollection and remembering are important aspects of preparing ourselves for risk and change. A summer friend may be the one who sees the need for ritual or one who suggests that we take time to focus the "I am, I can, I will" of self. Seeing the need for ritual is a priestly role, and it can be done for one another within the energy field of a summer friendship.

Even though it has been more than ten years since I went to the Faith at Work event which my summer friend Lura encouraged me to attend, I can still remember the preparation ritual of deciding what clothes to pack. It was March in Kansas and the weather was raw. I was used to wearing clay-spattered jeans in my pottery studio but, knowing this would be a church-related gathering, I bought a nice pair of wool slacks and a kelly-green wool shirt to wear over a turtle-neck sweater. The pants were a size smaller than I normally wore, because I had lost some weight in the months prior to going: I had stopped using food to satisfy a deeper craving that had no name yet.

I wanted to look casual and still appropriate, so I talked to Lura about the clothes I was planning to take, and her approval was important as I packed for the trip. Although I had traveled to Asia and South America by myself, I sensed the importance of this decision to leave Peter in Leavenworth for a week and go just three hours away to this Faith at Work event. I knew I was searching for something that had to do with combining my inward life with my outward role in the church. The ritual of selecting clothes was my preparation for a journey into the unknown, and the process symbolized my decision to heed Lura's vision.

Journal Questions
Preparation

- Identify a major turning point in your recent past and describe a summer friend who helped you prepare for it. What did your friend say or do?

- What clothing or other objects were symbols of your preparation ritual?

- How did you share that turning point with your summer friend?

Discovery

Summer friends recognize their differences and operate independently. Like polar opposites in a magnetic field, summer friends are related by common interests or common goals, but they may repel each other when forced together. Each must feel free to choose their times of intimacy and vulnerability. Because of their essential separateness, discovery of a deeper current between summer friends may come as a surprise or even a shock of spiritual connection.

When Ruth decided to approach Boaz on the threshing floor, she claimed her own power to risk life and death. Naomi could not do it for her. Although Ruth had undertaken a similar journey by day when she had gone into the barley fields the first time, she was entering a more highly-charged field this time. Even though the darkness gave her some protection, she would not be able to see Boaz and might approach the wrong man. And if she found Boaz, he might not agree to do what she asked: he might not be willing to interrupt village customs in order to redeem the two women.

Following the meal which Boaz shared with the other harvesters, Ruth noticed where he lay down for the night. When it was dark, she went to him, uncovered his feet, and lay down as Naomi had directed. Whether uncovering his feet was a biblical euphemism for nakedness or sexual intercourse, or simply an act that would cause him to stir in his sleep to find a warm covering again, it signified Ruth's active invitation to intimacy.

According to Naomi's direction, Boaz would tell Ruth what to do when he awakened: all she had to do was to begin their interaction. But when Boaz woke in the night to find a woman lying at his feet, he did not tell her what to do. Instead he asked, "Who are you?"

Suddenly Ruth was in the position of accepting her power and presence there. She was not simply an agent of Naomi's scheme, nor a lonely woman looking for comfort after too much wine. She had prepared herself in a ritual way for this engagement. She had come to ask for help, to seek a path of survival for herself and Naomi.

"I am your servant Ruth," she answered with her own name, "Spread the corner of your garment over me, since you are a kinsman-redeemer" (3:9). The image of spreading his garment over her recalled the reference to finding refuge beneath the wings of God which Boaz had invoked when they first met

(2:12). Once again Ruth had chosen into God's favor by her own volition. Answering with her own name and a clear, straightforward request defined her separate identity: I am Ruth. She told Boaz what to do, not the other way around. She took the initiative to get the favor that she and Naomi wanted.

When Ruth called Boaz a kinsman-redeemer, she identified a role for him that still belonged to the future. It would require his cooperation and a favorable judgment by the city elders. The purpose of redemption among the Hebrews was to secure the property of a family by providing a male heir. And since conception was thought to be a gift of God, by inviting Boaz to conceive a child with her, Ruth was not only claiming the right to provide a male heir for Naomi but was claiming the power of Naomi's God as well. Against the backdrop of her childless marriage to Naomi's son Mahlon, Ruth's whispered invitation to Boaz was also a confession of faith!

In response to Ruth's words, Boaz revealed his own vulnerability. "Bless you, my daughter," the aging man replied, "for this last act of kindness of yours is greater than the first, since you have not gone after young men, poor or rich" (3:10 JB). In Boaz' mind, Ruth's first act of kindness had been her decision to leave her homeland and accompany Naomi on the dangerous journey to Bethlehem. Now he saw her choice to approach him instead of a younger man or nearer relative as another act of kindness. Ruth's honesty evoked his own. Her invitation brought him hope. Boaz came down off his pedestal of authority and control and with his words, "Bless you, my daughter," he let Ruth know that they were mutually involved in redeeming life for each other.

Boaz concluded this part of the story by committing himself to do what Ruth asked of him. "Have no fear then," Boaz said, "I will do whatever you ask, for the people of Bethlehem all know your worth" (3:12 JB). With these words, Boaz made an unconditional commitment to be guided by Ruth. From his stance within the community of Bethlehem, he guessed that he would succeed in his effort to redeem Ruth and Naomi, but his response suggested that he was also sensitive to the chance Ruth had taken. Perhaps he remembered Rahab, his foremother, in a similar night-time encounter and wanted to reassure Ruth that her safety and her future were important to him.

In response to Boaz' question, "Who are you?," Ruth was able to discover more of her call and identity. Just as she had been free to make an earlier commitment to Naomi, she could deal with the surprising openness of Boaz when he did not tell her what to do. She could meet him as a summer friend, very different in age and status, and be clear about her choice to be with him. When he asked her to stay the night and return to Naomi at dawn, she did. As summer friends, they each brought different needs to the spectrum of their relationship: maturity and aging, woman and man, poverty and wealth. Through their differences Ruth and Boaz were linked: their separate needs connected to further God's larger story, and their meeting gave each of them the courage to say "Yes" to the possibilities of new life!

As women, we are socialized *not* to ask "Who am I?" We are encouraged to find an identity as somebody's daughter, wife, or mother. But a summer friend will persist in probing, "Who are you?" The answer to that question depends upon hearing the call to be alive as an individual and then acting from that center. Sometimes discovering who "I am" means leaving the roles that defined us previously: daughter, wife, mother, even friend. Being centered in one's own body and being clear about who "I am" is essential for the kind of freedom to make commitments that Ruth displayed with Naomi and with Boaz.

Because of the polarity between summer friends, they are particularly helpful in the process of defining the "I am" of an individual. The differences between summer friends are likely to be obvious—as with Ruth and Boaz—which makes fusion impossible. Summer friends bring diversity, energy, and occasionally clashing interests to their relationships. A summer friend is one who respects the boundaries of individuality, welcomes differences as creative potential, and is protective of the other's dignity. A summer friend will help to pose the questions, "Who are you?" and "Who are you becoming?," without trying to determine the answer.

In my own life, the seasons of friendship cycled once again when we moved from Leavenworth, Kansas, to the Washington, D.C., area. Once again I was restless to take another step on my spiritual journey of discovering my call toward some kind of ministry. When I was invited to be on the leadership team for a Faith at Work event similar to the one I had experienced in Kansas, I was glad to be asked and looked forward to meeting the others who would be on the team. When we got to the retreat center, I discovered that all six of us, men and women, were in some kind of transition at work or at home. I anticipated an exciting and stimulating week.

Midway through the week, I was shocked into relationship by the incredible vulnerability of another woman. My journal recorded our meeting this way:

> . . . deep sobs—I stood in the bathroom doorway, afraid of what I might see. When I went in, Marianne was gripping the sink, crying from her belly with her head against the mirror. I put my arm around her and felt her sag.
>
> "Would you hold me?"
>
> "Yes."
>
> I felt terrified. What would she need?
>
> "Take your contacts out and let me get a cold cloth for your eyes."
>
> She did and we went to my room. We lay down on the bed together, and I held her while she cried and cried. In bits and pieces the story came: her fourth child had died in childbirth ten years before. She had almost bled to death. When she "came to," the child was gone, unnamed and unknown. She had buried the memory to get on with her life. Now the memory had surfaced: it was the anniversary of the baby's death.

Our friendship began with Marianne's grief and my response. Our connection was at the level of being, deeper than words. The intensity of her emotion was frightening and holy at the same time. Previously, I had only seen the responsible elder sister and the playful child in Marianne. Now there was no escape into easy banter: I could not ignore the depth of what we had shared, the risk of her trust in my stability and vulnerability. Like Ruth, I was able to walk through my fears. Instead of holding back out of my fear of touch and emotion, I was able to be present to Marianne's horror of losing a child and nearly losing her own life as well. Even though I could not identify with her experience, I discovered courage and responsiveness I did not know that I had. Later, she said that my physical presence without judgment or advice had provided safety and time for the memories to surface.

Journal Questions
Discovery

- When have you met a summer friend by entering a new or frightening situation?
- What did you discover about yourself in that encounter?
- How did that experience affect your friendship?

Full-fillment

Intentional risks with another person provoke new possibilities, generate new promises, and may produce effects which were not anticipated by either person. If these risks grow out of a search for life beyond survival, then moments of extreme vulnerability can produce change beyond the encounter of two individuals. Preparation is integrated, discoveries are made, and spiritual hungers are filled.

As the night waned, Boaz responded to Ruth's initiative from his own place within the cultural system of Bethlehem. He protected Ruth by rousing her "before the hour when one man can recognize another, for . . . it must not be known that this woman came to the threshing floor" (3:15 JB). He was aware that Ruth could have been molested or stoned if the other men discovered her there. He also recognized the danger of community censure because their nighttime liaison was beyond the limits of cultural approval. Protecting her reputation with the townspeople was important to the negotiations that lay ahead of him.

The image of Boaz and Ruth lying together on the threshing floor raises the issue of touch in our friendships. The intensity and polarity of summer friendships often contain sexual energy like that between Boaz and Ruth. Sharing new aspects of self, whether inward or outward, can generate strong feelings of attraction and intimacy between two people. Without the conservative safeguards of a community context, that bi-polar attraction can and does release explosive energy which can, in turn, destroy old patterns of loyalty. There will indeed be "intercourse" in a summer friendship: intense exchange and communication, but not necessarily the fusion of coitus. Acknowledging sexual energy and channeling it toward the functional goals of a summer friendship can bring a dynamic kind of synergy to a relationship that will be missing in other seasons.

Too often in our culture, the aspect of touch is missing from friendship because of our sexual fears. We end up limiting the level of intimacy to words and common activities, reserving touch for the marriage bed or casual sex. Some of our culture's compulsive sex may well come from the inhibitions we have about common forms of touching and holding. Perhaps we can re-discover our ability to touch in the privacy of a summer friendship which releases us to be more open, more vulnerable, more truthful about who we are and what we need.

As Ruth prepared to leave the threshing floor, Boaz filled her cloak with six measures of barley as a sign to Naomi that he would be their kinsman-redeemer. Once again, Boaz answered Naomi's physical hunger with food. At a literal level, both Ruth and Naomi were "full-filled" by the grain gift as a sign that Ruth had successfully accomplished her mission. At a symbolic level, Boaz provided a sign of fulfillment for Naomi's and Ruth's spiritual hunger. By implication, the food was a sign of God's on-going presence and protection in Ruth's journey of risk and courage. The grain signified Boaz' pledge to act on their behalf in the area where he had power and credibility. And at a metaphorical level, the whole interaction conveyed the essence of a summertime interaction: initiative, independence, self-identity, bi-polar energy, and a commitment to be in relationship while acting separately.

Naomi responded with satisfaction to Ruth's account of what had happened, saying, "Wait. . .and see how things will go, for he will not rest until it is settled" (3:18 JB). Although Ruth and Boaz were the principal actors in this scene of the story, Naomi began and ended their encounter with her words. She was the prophetic voice, interpreting events from God's larger perspective. She had seen the signs of God's provision during the spring season of their relationship while Ruth was working in the fields. She had dared to face the possibility of famine as summer came and to find a new pathway so both of them could live.

As summertime friends, Naomi and Ruth, and Ruth and Boaz, had to work separately, each with a piece of the larger plan to accomplish: Naomi, with her vision of finding a place for her and Ruth in Bethlehem; Ruth, with her courage to take action; and Boaz, with his commitment to open the closed system of Bethlehem.

The encounter between Ruth and Boaz changed everything for the two women, but they could do nothing to hurry the chain of reactions that would fill the need which had initially prompted Naomi's daring plan. They had to wait for Boaz to begin the process that would accomplish Naomi's dream.

The issue of fulfillment in my own life centered around a question of call and vocation as I approached midlife. After twenty years of marriage, Peter represented the conservative context of past expectations and on-going obligations—village values. Like Naomi, my new summer friend Marianne held a vision for my call to ministry. The Boaz I had to approach was internal and remote: the phantom male voice that would keep me a dependent girl instead of an independent woman. I needed to gather my courage, approach my internal Boaz through a maze of other potential diversions, and name my self when the question came, "Who are you?"

Marianne was my Naomi for this phase of my inner journey, holding out a vision for my place in the public realm of church ministry. The week-long event where we met ended with a closing called "dreaming the future." The image I had of God's call was that of an itinerant teacher, moving from one group to another, speaking, sharing, and inviting others to share their faith stories. Marianne confirmed that call and agreed to hold it with me in prayer.

During this season of our friendship, neither one of us needed a friend who would take a lot of time and attention. Marianne was in graduate school in Chicago, and I had a full-time pottery business in Alexandria, Virginia. It was probably no accident that we lived a thousand miles apart. We each had the inner resources necessary for our separate and separating paths, but it felt like a gift from God to have someone else to talk with who was not invested in preserving old patterns of home and family.

In the next few years, my friendship with Marianne deepened as she helped me to recognize and name my gifts for teaching and preaching. She was not afraid of touch and emotional intimacy. We attended retreats and conferences together, as I confronted the inner fears that would keep me homebound. She gave me a place to stay, made my visits a celebration of food and talk, and mentored my emerging gifts into being.

Her support and encouragement was important for me as I made the jump from being a full-time professional potter into providing learning experiences for church groups. She walked with me as a sister, as a midwife, and as a summer friend, helping me realize my dream and bring home my own "grain sign" of fulfillment—working in ministry with Faith at Work.

Journal Questions
Full-fillment

- Can you identify someone who challenges you to grow without invading your space? Who? How?

- Does that relationship bring "new life" to you in some way?

- What are the difficulties that your summer friendship creates at home? Or among old friends?

5. Autumn Friendship:
Entering Community

Naomi dreamed
 of how it
 was when she was young:
  a community of women
   around the village well.
  Her dream now a vision
 of moving from
 summer singularity
to autumn web of "us" with Bethlehem.

From threshing floor to city gate
 Boaz came
 to intercede for them —
  bargain before the elders
   as redeemer.
  The kinsman with prior claim
 said "yes" to land
 but "no" to Ruth
so Boaz made his move:

he would restore Elimelech's line
 (though in the end
 his name joined Ruth's
  as forebears of David
   . . . and Jesus)
  by buying Naomi's land
 and with it Ruth.
 The other man withdrew;
the elders then agreed.

In spiritual communion
 the women sang the mythic tale

. . . of Rachel and Leah
foremothers of Israel
(envious sisters. . .
one beloved;
the other more fruitful)
married to Jacob, the cheat,
long before Egypt and Exodus;

. . . naming Ruth
more valuable
than seven sons,
a foremother of Israel;
one of "us."

Vision

Autumn friendships are embedded in community with
many surrounding relationships, both chosen and given by birth.
What is singular and special in summertime becomes plural and
plentiful in the autumn season of friendship. Groups absorb the
energy and diffuse direction of summer friends, integrating
individuality with traditions and customs. Community provides
a field of other options and obligations in which friendship can
either grow or wither: rules, roles, and mythic interpretation mark
the shift from summer to autumn. Community norms pervade
actions and words as friends are integrated or separated from
the on-going stream of village values. Either a community must
have a value system that is ready to receive newcomers who
don't fit the norms, or the shift from summer singularity to
autumn community requires someone inside the community
structure to serve as a bridge person, someone like Boaz to "sit
at the gate."

Naomi's long-range vision for entering the social fabric of
Bethlehem was expansive, inclusive, and full of autumn
abundance. She saw that God's provision was already including
herself and Ruth, so her wait for Boaz to act had not been in
vain. Though she did not have the power to accomplish her
vision alone, or even with the help of Ruth, she had set into

motion the forces that would eventually make them part of the community.

Naomi knew that Boaz understood the power structure within the city walls. Earlier in the story, when he had asked his foreman about Ruth, inquiring "Whose woman is that?," Boaz had spoken as one with control over the lives of others, an owner acquainted with money and property, a thinking man of the city. Naomi made a choice for Boaz over any nearer kinsman, perhaps because she recognized in Boaz a man who was also sensitive to God's presence beyond the city walls of Bethlehem. Naomi valued the kindness which Boaz had shown to Ruth when she first went out to the fields alone.

Naomi's vision was brought into focus at the gate where Boaz would meet the elders. The presence of a gate implied the presence of a wall around Bethlehem marking the boundaries, containing those who belonged, and excluding those who did not. The gate was the nexus of city and countryside where customs and laws of the city touched the natural rhythms of the countryside. Like the mouth of a communal body, the gate was a place where the flow of commerce in goods and people could be managed and directed, sorting who should be admitted and who should be kept out.

Having just completed his own harvest in the fields, Boaz came to the city gate for another kind of harvest. He was prepared to wait for the man who had first claim on Elimelech's property so they could negotiate a redemption agreement in front of the elders. As a farmer who had watched patiently for his own crops to ripen, Boaz had learned the discipline of waiting for God's timing.

In a sense, Boaz himself was a gateway to community for the women. Ruth could not traverse community boundaries alone; she could not make "your people" into "my people" by herself. Ruth's work had been effective in the fields where her labor and industry could be seen and appreciated. There Boaz could use his community status to provide protection for her. But when the harvest ended, Boaz could not "spread his wings over her" without drawing her inside the legal system of the community, where the laws and customs for insiders would protect her when his personal power was not enough or was gone. Naomi's vision and Boaz' action were both essential in order for the two women to enter the covenantal fabric of Bethlehem.

Today, a real community is hard to find, and access to a community is no easier to accomplish for us than it was for Ruth. At work, we substitute association and common tasks for community, like field workers in the Ruth story. Generally, we do not experience the mutual accountability of a creative social organism in the work place. At home, in the nomadic culture of modern America, we often live in isolation or we try to make a marriage with children into a community because there isn't time or place for more. Common leisure activities may give the appearance of community, because people do the same thing at the same time in the same place, but mutual commitment is missing.

In our transient neighborhoods, churches provide one possibility for community, but people must do more than come every Sunday and sit in straight rows in order to make that potential into a functional reality. And if, like city walls, there are dogmatic boundaries which define a church community, then someone must have Naomi's vision to look for an interpreter for newcomers. Access would still depend upon a bridge person like Boaz at the gate who would love and serve the outsider or the stranger into the common life of the community.

Many of us never experience autumn friendships because we do not have the community context suggested by that season. Instead, we isolate a spring friendship at home and perhaps develop a summer friendship or two at work. But without a community to expand and develop those friendships, our relationships sour or become boring and then, in desperation, we trade one partner for another. The full cycle of seasonal friendships does not develop because the modern American cultural context has destroyed the community that once was defined by a village economy and a common church. Unless we learn to "re-invent community" as a consciously chosen extended family, we will not experience the abundance and richness of autumn friendships.

Initially, most of us do what Ruth did: we separate home and work. We find a partner to maintain a home with some companionship in it, and we find a work place with enough safety for survival. As we grow, however, we may experience a yearning that cannot be filled by singular friendships. If we develop community with existing friends, access is not a problem because the boundaries are not firm. But if, as strangers, we approach an on-going body of people, then we face the same problem of entry with which Ruth and Naomi had to cope: we have to find a way into the value system and on-going stories that bind a community together.

In my own life, the summer season of friendship shifted dramatically into autumn after Peter retired from the Army and we moved back to Washington, D.C., from a tour in Germany. Although we were coming back to a known house and circle of friends at the church, we had changed. Our separate vocational needs were quite different now that we did not expect to move again. When we lived in D.C. before, the church had provided a substitute family for both Peter and me. This time, I was clear about wanting support for some particular form of ministry as we entered the community once again. Peter was also open to guidance and direction in his choice of work. We were both looking for an autumn community where friendships from other seasons could be integrated more fully.

The first gate into community that I recognized opened into Seekers, one of the six little churches in The Church of the Saviour. That community had clear boundaries, defined by the membership commitment which we had left when we went to Germany. The person who became my bridge into that community once again was not yet a member herself. She was actively involved and accepted by Seekers, and she helped me to see that I did not have to join the membership circle in order to be welcome. Lewise sought a friendship with me outside of church by setting up a weekly time to do something together. Then, as part of the same mission group, we prayed, shared spiritual disciplines, and worked on the adult education program together every week. Her wry questions and psychologist's background helped me clarify my motives for re-joining the members.

Through my friendship with Lewise, I began to see that I really wanted to be ordained to ministry. . .I just didn't know what form that ministry would take and, therefore, who the confirming community would be. One of the next gates that opened to me was into Faith at Work, a "city" with loose boundaries and open membership. This ecumenical organization, which had been so important to me in Kansas and again in Virginia, was in flux when we returned from Germany. The new ministry for women had lost its organizational leader when the paid staff was cut in 1982, so I asked the Board if I could work as the volunteer coordinator for the women's ministry for two years. Lewise affirmed my initiative by intentionally choosing to attend a Faith at Work Women's Event which I was leading.

To test my call even further, I started seminary as a half-time student. As the wife of a seminary faculty member, Lewise invited me to stop by for coffee on the days when I was taking classes. She gave me a place to explore the connections between Seekers and Faith at Work. Like Naomi, Lewise held out a vision for ministry in a larger, complex community. Through our discussions, I began to see that the community of Seekers— with its clear boundaries and written rules for membership— was like a walled city within the broader community of Faith at Work. My autumn friendship with Lewise helped me to see the whole picture of my place in these overlapping communities.

Journal Questions
Vision

- Draw a shape that represents your gifts.

- Add a circle representing a walled city (or cities) where you would like to put your gifts to work.

- Mark a gate (or several) and name an autumn friend who helps you see the whole picture.

- How does your autumn friend hold out a larger vision for you?

Intercession

Engaging the power and authority structures in "the city" is the second step of entering community. There are always elders who guard the history, the customs, the boundaries, and the property of a corporate body. Finding a place within the structure may be as simple as learning the jargon and the rules that govern the activities of a particular group—like dressing appropriately or knowing where to park. But finding a place among the power brokers or entering the leadership circle can be much more difficult. Access to "the city" requires an intercessor who is recognized by the elders. People like Ruth and Naomi who are outside of the power structure need someone like Boaz to intercede for them.

The elders of Bethlehem met near the city gate. As in many warm climates, they probably squatted informally in a circle where they could watch the traffic and trade, exchange gossip, and make whatever rulings were needed to safeguard the orderly patterns of life in the village. By Jewish law, ten men constituted a legal body: the elders represented power and authority in the community. Because they could make legally binding judgments, they had the power to release the first claimant of Elimelech's family from the option of redeeming Naomi and Ruth. When the first claimant (who remained unnamed throughout this encounter) did appear at the gate, Boaz invited him to sit down with ten elders.

Then Boaz introduced a new piece of information to the story by revealing that Naomi wanted to sell a piece of land which had belonged to Elimelech. Since married women did not normally participate in property ownership among the Jews, Naomi may not have known, when she first arrived in Bethlehem, that she had something to sell. But Boaz knew about the land, and when he spoke, Naomi suddenly attracted the attention of the elders because she had worth and value in the city economy. Offering Naomi's land for sale provided Boaz with a negotiating position in the property ownership system that the men controlled, but it also meant that Naomi and Ruth were no longer invisible to the men of Bethlehem. The elders were forced to consider Naomi's future now that Boaz had raised the issue of her property ownership.

Although Boaz offered Naomi's land to the unnamed first claimant, he made a clear statement of his intention to redeem the land if the man did not want to buy it from Naomi. However, this man, who had not come forward to redeem Naomi when she had first returned from Moab, was now interested in acquiring the land. He agreed to buy Naomi's field, perhaps expecting a bargain from the poor widow who had been absent from Bethlehem most of her adult life.

Then Boaz added a crucial bit of information: "On the day you purchase the land from Naomi, you purchase Ruth the Moabitess also. . .and so restore [Elimelech's] name to his inheritance" (4:5 JB). Upon hearing of Ruth's inclusion in the deal, the man retracted his claim. He did not want to jeopardize his own line of inheritance by the possibility of another claimant to his wealth, should Ruth conceive and bear a son. No mention was made of her ten-year marriage or lack of conception with Mahlon: the men simply assumed that Ruth would bear a child and so restore the family to its place in the community. There was no wonder, no mystery, no questioning of God's hand in their deliberations: it was an economic question based on property ownership, resource control, and inheritance.

Ruth was a complicating factor for the nearest kinsman. If he had acted on his own when Naomi had first returned, as the first claimant from Elimelech's clan he might have received Naomi's land without her awareness and simply sent Ruth back to Moab as a foreigner with no legal claim. That clearly had been Naomi's understanding of the situation when she had originally urged both of the Moabite wives to return to their homes: she did not foresee land ownership as access to the community in Bethlehem. But now Boaz pressed the claim to Elimelech's property by linking Ruth with Naomi's land, and in so doing, Boaz provided legitimacy for Ruth which the younger woman could not have gained for herself.

For us, the path toward a chosen community may be quite similar to Ruth's. Our parents may have provided some place, position, or status for us in a childhood community. We carry that image of community, colored by our feelings about parents and home, into adulthood. Then, like Ruth, we leave home, land, family, or other inheritance—and often a childhood image of God as well. We live through one or more seasonal cycles, finding a spring or summer friend to share a phase or season. Some may find entrance to an autumn community an easy, natural process that develops from the ripening fruits of each season. But others of us may not be ready to enter community for fear that our summer individuality will be engulfed by autumn conviviality. Yet a longing for connection may draw us homeward again, whether that means to a physical place (like Naomi) or a spiritual home (like Ruth). In either case, we will have to find a redeemer from within the community to act as an intercessor.

Many women may expect marriage to provide enough community for adult life, but usually that pairing is too constricted for a full cycle of friendship. Marriage itself belongs to springtime, where it can provide safety, nurture, and dialogue. A marriage may survive the summer periods of stretching and growth, but then autumn brings more options for community: a richer mixture of people in diverse relationships to support and extend a primary pairing if there is one. When the time comes for a woman to engage with the money or property system of her culture, she will usually need an intercessor from "the city" she wants to enter, an autumn friend who understands the power structure of that community.

In each of the two communities that I began to enter after we returned to Washington, D.C., a redeemer appeared just when I needed someone to be in that intercessory position. In the Seekers community, one of the pastors became a redeemer when she invited me to rest, to wait, to take on no special roles for a while. Sonya cautioned me to stop and listen for God's call instead of filling my time with activities. Although there were jobs I could have done, she urged me to "watch the traffic" and pray for the right time to pass through the gate into membership again. She legitimized my re-entry process.

In the community of Faith at Work, an unexpected redeemer appeared. Within the organizational structure of Faith at Work, the board of directors functioned as "the elders." Among the board members, I was recognized for the work that I was doing in the women's ministry, but one particular woman became my intercessor, advocating that my volunteer status as coordinator of the women's ministry become a paid job one day a week. Through her position on the board, she gave me access to the power structure which I could not earn as a volunteer— it could only be given by "the elders" by making the circle of leadership bigger. Nell interceded for me, but it took the cooperation of the other board members to widen the circle and give me a legitimate place on the staff.

By providing access to the inner workings of two different communities, both Nell and Sonya legitimized my call to ministry. The process of negotiating the terms by which I could enter the larger "outer city" of Faith at Work through Nell's friendship, and the smaller "inner city" of Seekers through Sonya's friendship, clarified my sense of God's call.

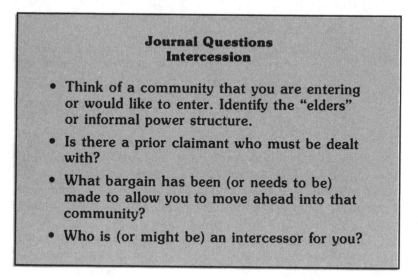

Journal Questions
Intercession

- **Think of a community that you are entering or would like to enter. Identify the "elders" or informal power structure.**

- **Is there a prior claimant who must be dealt with?**

- **What bargain has been (or needs to be) made to allow you to move ahead into that community?**

- **Who is (or might be) an intercessor for you?**

Confirmation

Transition into the communal relations of autumn is often accompanied by signs which mark our release from prior claims and open the way to expanding new roles and relationships in the community. As we enter community and recognize the formal or informal structure of power and control, the question of being received becomes more acute. Finally, the community itself must provide some act of confirmation if we are to feel at home there. Often that means being included in the stories or mythology by which a community describes itself.

In the biblical story, when Boaz agreed to purchase the land and Ruth in front of ten elders from the town, the transaction was completed when the first claimant removed his sandal and gave it to Boaz. The leather sandal, marked with this man's footprint, was a sign that would stand as evidence before tribal judges if there was some question about the agreement with Boaz. When the elders acknowledged the transaction, they recognized the property relationship between Naomi and Ruth and approved the place which the women would both have as part of Boaz' household. From being just a simple shield for the wearer's feet, the sandal became a sign of relinquishment for the first claimant and a sign of community inclusion by law for Ruth and Naomi.

After the men completed their legal transaction, the village women gave it a mythic interpretation by offering their communal blessing to the marriage of Ruth and Boaz: "May Yahweh make the woman who is to enter your House like Rachel and Leah who together built up the House of Israel" (4:11 JB). Their words were a song of confirmation, now that Ruth had completed her long journey from one community to another—from her marriage in Moab to a new one in Bethlehem, accompanied all the way by Naomi.

Invoking the Genesis story of Rachel and Leah (Genesis 29-30) was also a ritual fertility blessing, inviting Yahweh to open Ruth's womb as it had not been before. The village women thus became the voice of historical blessing for Ruth's entry into the community. Rachel and Leah had not only provided Jacob with many sons (thus becoming foremothers of Israel), but their fecundity had provided Jacob with a sign of God's blessing which ultimately gave him courage to confront his guilt for cheating his elder brother, Esau, out of their father's blessing

(Genesis 33). Although Boaz was not "cheating" his elder brother, he did in fact usurp the place of Mahlon and Elimelech in the "house and lineage of David" (Matthew 1:5). So God's blessing in this story, as in many others in the Old Testament, did not depend upon pure blood-lines or good behavior, so much as it depended upon Ruth's openness to God's leading, through Naomi, into the community of Israel.

The women's story contained another curious reference to God's presence in their community: "Through the offspring the Lord gives you by this young woman, may your family be like that of Perez, whom Tamar bore to Judah" (4:12). The story of Judah and Tamar, Elimelech's ancestors, was another tale of tangled genealogy, in which Tamar tricked her father-in-law, Judah, into fathering her child (actually twins) after her own husband had died and his brother Onan "spilled his seed on the ground" rather than preserve his brother's line through Tamar (Genesis 38). The blessing of the village women thus celebrated Tamar for her ingenuity and named her the carrier of God's blessing through Elimelech's family line. The women were more concerned about fertility than who fathered the children; they celebrated the clan and community more than individual ownership.

The man's sandal and the women's song represent two kinds of confirmation given by the Bethlehem community. The men focused on control and property, what belonged to "me and mine," and the sandal exchange was a sign of Ruth's inclusion under Mosaic Law. The women spoke with the communal voice of "us and ours," and their song included Ruth in the on-going story of their people. Ruth's relationship to Boaz under the Law was set in the larger circle of God's movement in history as the story was interpreted and told by the women. Invoking the stories of Rachel and Leah, Tamar and Judah, the women recalled the mysterious ways in which God had worked through property and ownership disputes in the past to bring vitality and new life to the covenant people. The women sang of the larger life-force pulsing through the community, and they directed their words to Naomi, as though to confirm her original hope and vision.

Both the legal structure and the mythic interpretation belong to the autumn season of friendship. In my own life, there was a legal symbol and a mythical song of community blessing. The sandal exchange occurred in December, 1985, when I became the new president of Faith at Work. For six months I had been running the office while a search committee looked for "a prior claimant" to the position. Traditionally, the job had been filled by a male clergyperson, and the committee examined a number of candidates before selecting me for the job. I also needed to examine my call to that position with the help of Sonya and others from my church community. But when the sandal was offered—when the job was clearly mine if I wanted it—I was ready to accept it.

Confirmation by a larger community came in a surprising and spontaneous way. When I began my leadership, there was no gathered community of Faith at Work: I simply continued going to the office as I had been for six months. My appointment would not be confirmed by the official "elders" until the board met several months later, and I felt disappointed. However, during a weekend Faith at Work Women's Event which coincided with the beginning of my new position, I was called out of the circle to sit in a chair while the women gathered around me for prayer. As each one prayed for my role in guiding Faith at Work, she placed a construction-paper hand on me: by the end, I had forty colorful hands stuck all over! It was a wonderful "laying on of hands" in the best religious tradition of ordaining one to ministry.

Appropriately, my autumn friend Lewise was part of that spontaneous ordination service, linking Seekers, seminary, and my call to Faith at Work. Like the women in Naomi's story, these women offered their blessing out of a longer time-frame and a larger vision of how God works in the world through people. Much later, I would receive a specific charge—with a plain white clerical stole—from the official board of Faith at Work. Both blessings—the legal "sandal" and the women's "song"—were important; both represented confirmation by the community I was entering.

Journal Questions
Confirmation

- Who has confirmed (or is confirming) your entrance into community?

- What symbols do you have of your acceptance into community?

- How does your community bless you?

6. Winter Friendship:
Sharing My Self

Wintertime
   season of "me" and "mine"
      solitude and stillness.

With child
   Ruth waited
      silent
            still
      alone
   drawing on her inner resources
sharing her body-self.

Her pledge
   to Naomi
      recalled
            relived
      reversed
   by Naomi
to Ruth.

"I Will Go Where You Go"

When external circumstances change and we plunge into the unknown realm of spirit, of mystery, of death and birth, then the commitment of a winter friend means sharing what, in other seasons, we keep to ourselves: the inner world of self. Dialogue beyond words takes on new meaning. Events are re-interpreted. The past is re-worked by reflecting on it, and interdependence becomes a living reality.

The friendship between Ruth and Naomi shifted from autumn to winter when Ruth married Boaz and they conceived a child. From the community interplay of legal discussion and mythic integration, Ruth withdrew into ritual seclusion and Naomi took charge of the new household, claiming her role as family matriarch. Few words are given in the biblical story to describe the winter season of Ruth's life: the narrator simply reported that "Yahweh made her conceive and she bore a son" (4:14 JB). But we know that nine months passed, and life for Ruth and Naomi would never be the same again.

The long gestation period was a time of stillness and darkness for the child whose very presence gave Ruth a new identity as a mother and shifted her relationship to Naomi, to Boaz, and to the community as well. It was a very different winter season from the unprotected trek which the two women had made together from Moab to Bethlehem. This time they could rest safely in winter solitude, turning inward, musing and pondering without many words; it was a time of solitary reflection, of sorting the past, and dreaming the future together.

Ruth, having once made the pledge to Naomi to "go where you go," was now in a position where that pledge could be reciprocated. This time it was Naomi's turn to go with Ruth— into the new territory of motherhood where the younger one had to go by faith and the older one by memory. The circumstances of their friendship were quite different from finding food for survival. This time they were getting used to a new home that would probably be theirs until one or the other died. They had time to explore a different way of walking together in their relationship before the child's birth would give objective reality to their mothering roles.

Naomi's experience of pregnancy would have been somewhat similar to what Ruth was facing, but the background for her pregnancy would have been quite different. Naomi had borne her sons as a young woman in her home community and then had been forced to leave Bethlehem with Elimelech just to survive. In contrast, Ruth was older, matured by events and decisions that followed a decade of childless marriage and widowhood, and was now living in a foreign land.

Unlike Naomi, Ruth had been free to make her own decision to leave her homeland. Her independence was marked by total separation from her mother, community, religion, land, and language when she decided to leave Moab and go with Naomi to Bethlehem. But now Ruth had to shift from the independence of working hard in the male world of the fields to the patient waiting for her child to come when it would.

So the two women entered Ruth's emerging motherhood together, each bringing their different life stages and experience to yet another winter season in their relationship. Their shared commitment—"I will go where you go"—is a winter statement of walking together, parallel but not joined, exploring some inward terrain with terror or wonder. Giving priority to a winter friendship takes more attention than other relationships because winter friends do not make demands, are not intrusive, and do not require constant reassurances. It is difficult in our culture to take the *time* just to be together. One way to tend a winter friendship is to go away together, to attend a retreat or conference where someone else will make decisions about schedule and meals, and you can simply be with your friend.

Sharing an inward journey with someone who does *not* happen to live with you takes discipline and communication. Exchanging poems, letters, drawings, or even songs, can speak from the depths of one to another. If we have no language for our winter waiting time, we may feel depressed or isolated. But if we understand that winter is a resting time—a pause between sounds, a space between forms, a time of letting go before life rises once again—then we can welcome the winter season and look for our winter friends.

If we have shared a winter cycle with someone once before, that friendship may revive when the season comes round again.

I've noticed that whenever my own life brushes against death in some way, I reach out for Marianne because I know that she will not laugh it off or recoil in disgust from my groping speech and frequent silences. I trust her not to hurt my deepest self, not to shame my naked soul. Our impulses to reach for the phone and call just to talk often reveal some deeper stream that is flowing beneath the surface of our words. Most recently that stream has been connected to the declining health of her parents and mine, and the changes that are coming with their process of dying.

Like Ruth's period of gestation, winter friendships can shelter new birth as it develops. Last summer, Marianne and I spent a week at Lake Michigan together. A summer storm made the lakeside cabin a refuge while waves lashed at the seawall and rain pelted the windows, surrounding us with primal sound and fury. She was studying for her psychology licensing exams, and I was writing parts of this book. We kept silence all morning, then donned our slickers and walked in the cold spray before finding a place for dinner and some conversation. We expected sunshine and relaxation, but we were chilled and damp all week. Somehow the weather was perfect for our winter friendship because it encouraged us to stay inside and be still together at a time when both of us were birthing new parts of ourselves.

Journal Questions
"I Will Go Where You Go"

- Name a winter friend with whom you feel safe enough to share your inner self.
- Nonverbally describe your friendship—with an image, colors, or drawing.
- What new parts of your life have been birthed in the shelter of this friendship?

"I Will Live Where You Live"

Living where another lives has a double meaning: sharing the same inner space and being alive together. Winter friends can do both. Discovering what brings life to our souls through interaction with another is characteristic of winter friendship. Sharing that nourishment means revealing one's very source of life, living in a spiritual womb-space together.

Ruth had once pledged to live wherever Naomi was going to live, but in the end Naomi joined Ruth in a place that Ruth provided through her marriage to Boaz. The two friends had endured hardship together; now they had to face plenty together. They were wrapped together in the same physical house and nourished by the same spiritual source. As Naomi realized her long-held dream of having another child through Ruth, would she be able to maintain her friendship with the younger woman?

Ruth's pregnancy drew her focus inward, to her own body. After ten years of childless marriage to Mahlon and the hard seasons of widowhood with Naomi, suddenly Ruth had the safety and comfort she had not known before. As the child grew silently within her, Ruth would have known approval and acceptance by the other women of the village. Yet, as an active and self-reliant woman, the gestation period must have been difficult for her because it was so unfamiliar. Resting and receiving were not the postures that Ruth had assumed before.

Naomi, too, was pregnant with new life. Instead of dying old and alone and poor, she was in the process of becoming a grandmother. . . something she had wanted very much. Throughout the period that the two women had spent in Bethlehem, Naomi had grown in speech and imagination, as though her own body were "waking up" once again. Because of Ruth's course of action, Naomi had really begun to live again. Now Naomi had tangible proof that her life and Elimelech's line were not going to be snuffed out after all. Together, Naomi and Ruth began to create a space in their relationship for the new life that was coming to each of them.

Like Ruth, we also turn inward to be "at home" in our bodies in the winter season of our lives. We pull away from friends and family, away from the extroverted communal activities of autumn periods to replenish the solitary wellsprings of the soul. Winter is an introverted season, although we may remain functional and gregarious in public.

Winter friends draw sustenance from a common spiritual source, sharing some purpose or mutual need. These friends may be widows who work together on a church project, or young women who share a first apartment in the city to keep expenses down. Or, like Ruth and Naomi when they walked between Moab and Bethlehem, winter friends may "live together" as they endure a common experience of hardship or share some inward pain.

In contrast to summer friendships, which are full of intense conversation and new activity, winter friends are more likely to share the sounds and smells of ordinary activity, like cooking meals, without putting their thoughts into words. While the boundaries of "you" and "me" are still distinct, as in summer friendships, the environment is different: winter friends have come inside and are contained by a surrounding spirit which provides nourishment for them both.

Living where another lives can be frightening as well as comforting, because the intention during this season is to be alone. My old friend Michael came to visit recently with a bag of books, poetry, and fables. He wanted to show them to me and share some of the images that seemed important, although he could hardly tell me why. I browsed silently through his stack of new titles, warmed by his wanting to share them, envious of the treasure trove that would feed his imagination for a long time. Occasionally he broke the silence to read a poem aloud, and we half-spoke through intimations of someone else's words. His visit felt familiar, easy, comfortable. He was "at home" in my kitchen, sharing that common and yet intimate space. He "lives where I live," and through our friendship I have come to trust a sense of shared womb-space, of being alive from the same source.

> **Journal Questions**
> **"I Will Live Where You Live"**
>
> - In quiet winter periods, how do you get in touch with what brings life to your soul?
> - How do you share that "alive space" with a winter friend? What are your feelings when you are with that friend?

"Your People Will Be My People"

Identifying "my people" is an extension and expansion of understanding "my self." When we internalize a sense of belonging to a community—belonging to their history and ultimately their highest values, or God—then we reach a level of security and internal freedom which may allow us to share that heritage with others. In fact, winter friends who share the same internal community can give birth to "a new people" out of their commitment to each other, rather than searching for admittance to an external community created by others.

At the physical level, Naomi's people would never be Ruth's people, but the child of Ruth and Boaz would make the younger woman part of Naomi's family heritage. The child would move Naomi's and Ruth's friendship from a chosen commitment into the primitive bonding of blood and family.

But at the spiritual level, Naomi's people were already Ruth's family. As her pregnancy developed, Ruth withdrew from the active community and went into seclusion under the care of other women, particularly Naomi. It was a time for developing her trust and faith in the Jewish tribal customs which she had long ago accepted through her commitment to Naomi. As she gave herself to Naomi's people and carried in her womb a child who belonged among them, images of her own mother and her own childhood may have surrounded her as well. It would have been a time for remembering the past and dreaming the future for herself and her child. Like an animal in hibernation, sharing the time and space with other women, Ruth herself became the integration of her past and her present. What she had intended with her will and her words—"your people will be my people"—was now becoming spirit and flesh.

In the beginning it had been Naomi who had spoken so fervently about having a child. Ruth had never voiced any particular interest in marriage or childbearing, although she had asked Boaz directly to redeem them. Unlike most of the women in that day, Ruth always seemed more independent, operating by force of will instead of fitting into the collective patterns of childbearing that Naomi wanted. Now Ruth was joined to Naomi's people by marriage and by birth, birthing herself among them through this child. There would be no going back now, even if Naomi died. The coming of the child meant that Naomi's people were Ruth's own.

As Naomi and Ruth nurtured new life in themselves, their love birthed a story of friendship that is a powerful image of chosen relationship. The two women conceived and bore a vision of life that gave their lives importance beyond bringing children into the world, beyond the vision of their culture. Their story "gives birth" to many people—particularly alien or aging women—who would otherwise be excluded from the covenant.

The intensity of a relationship between winter friends will often give birth to something new, to a mythical child. That child is a "third party" to the relationship, giving shape and form to "a people" belonging to both partners. The mythical child could be as simple as acknowledging shared spirit-space or as complex as building a life together. As we become conscious of depth connections in our winter friendships, we may need to name and celebrate the mythical children of the relationship who give form and substance to "our people" in the world.

When I consider the question of mingling internal communities, I come back to my relationship with Peter, who is both my husband and often a winter friend. The mythical child, that "third party" of our relationship, has been conceived, birthed, sheltered, taught, and released into the unknown future as our relationship has matured. Sharing the same space at home and the same bed at night encourages our winter bond. Working and playing together has given birth to images that carry us through other seasons in our relationship.

I have learned that there is a big difference between saying the words of Ruth's pledge—"your people will be my people"—and living the words together. When I first said this pledge at our wedding, I took the words literally to mean that Peter's people would *replace* my own: his name would replace the one I had grown up with, his parents would substitute for mine, and his work would provide our community context. And, in some ways, that happened. However, over the years the deeper spiritual source of our winter friendship has provided a sense of belonging to a larger family than either his parents or mine, and we have shared the essence of our relationship as we have opened our home to others, creating "our people" in the process. Instead of having community made for us by others, we are birthing community out of our winter friendship.

Journal Questions
"Your People Will Be My People"

- **What has been born of your dreaming with a winter friend?**
- **How do you contribute to a "new people" or a new community out of a winter friendship?**

"Your God Will Be My God"

Entering someone else's belief system means sharing thoughts and values behind the descriptive words and stories of their faith. But the covenant faith goes even further to say that one can actually be in relationship with Yahweh, the living God. Beyond the Mosaic Law, God is understood to be the source of life—a central "I am who I am" (Exodus 3:14).

If Naomi's God had blessed the marriage of Ruth and Boaz by causing Ruth to conceive this child, then Ruth's faithful pursuit of this redeeming act had brought Naomi back to a living relationship with the covenant again. Following the death of her two sons, Naomi had felt cursed by God, or at least felt that God's blessing had been withdrawn from her family. Naomi's core of faith had been stripped of all wish-dreams to a simple act of will—choosing life—in order to make the long desert journey from Moab to Bethlehem. Now her faith took on flesh and blood once again with the blessing of the child in Ruth's womb.

Ruth, too, must have felt God's blessing on her union with Boaz when she conceived a child so quickly. But as she became part of the covenant people through this child, she also knew that her full acceptance by them lay in bearing a son, not a daughter, to continue Elimelech's line. Unlike nearby goddess-worshipping tribes (like the Canaanites), Israel was a patriarchal society, and the historical focus was on having male descendants. Fertility rites and household gods were rejected by the priests and judges of Israel, although the Hebrews did regard fecundity as a sign of Yahweh's presence and provision for them. It was the historical dimension that made Naomi's God different from the household gods with whom Ruth probably grew up. Now Ruth was entering the chain of historical record through her child.

For women today, the Judeo-Christian preference for males continues to be a stumbling block for many. The idea that Ruth's importance to God's story through the people of Israel rests on the gender of her child is repugnant to us because it implies that women are only valuable if they bear children, especially male children. However, the story of Ruth is much more than a name in a genealogical list. The complexity of the story of her relationship with Naomi suggests that God's presence was being carried and nurtured by the two women as they lived through the changing seasons of friendship together. Ruth's story reveals a God of relationship who goes far beyond the literal birth of a child and the gender preference of a people.

The friendship between Ruth and Naomi actually is a dynamic portrayal of the nature of God: inviting, inclusive and expansive. This God joins Ruth and Naomi, drawing them toward life before the older woman was even conscious of the bonding between them. This God beckons Ruth with an invitation to faithful commitment, rather than subservient sacrifice. This God responds to the independent choice of a "foreigner." This God is quite beyond the conventional images of a patriarchal Old Testament judge. The God revealed by this story is rooted in the history of the Israelites, but not confined to their cultural expression.

Like Ruth, we can learn the substance of a relationship with God through the discipline of a committed friendship. At different times in Ruth's and Naomi's relationship, one supplied what the other could not. Without the perseverance and physical energy of Ruth, they might not have survived. Without the vision of Naomi, the provision of God might have gone unnoticed. We, too, need the different gifts that individuals bring to a relationship. We need the different perspectives of age and experience. Through our differences, we bring our combined life experience, positive and negative, to the words of faith recorded in the Bible, and then we begin to understand the meaning and purpose and interconnection of all life. We catch sight of God's vision for the diversity of creation and for the part that we have in it.

Finding a relationship with God through a friendship is yet another step beyond walking together or living together. I think of my young friend Sarah who has difficulty being still: she is an extroverted real estate agent with a long history of working with youth groups in church. We met at a crisis time in her life when none of the answers she had grown up with worked any more. At a women's retreat, she said simply, "Tell me about your God."

Sarah had enough faith in me to ask. I wanted to give her a descriptive answer. Doctrine would not do. Dogma was too abstract. At a nonverbal level, she sensed that something was feeding my inner life, and she needed new words that would help her name her inner experience. I described my awareness of God in everyday images. I knew that my God was already her God, but she did not have the language for that yet. I listened hard for the inward stream that would quench her thirst while I spoke to her questioning mind. In today's culture, we live with such a Greek linguistic split between body and spirit that I felt myself reaching back into history for some Hebrew "soul talk," where God was present in biblical stories. In the end, I used Ruth's and Naomi's story to describe the God of relationship, the God of Rachel and Leah, of Tamar . . . and of Sarah and myself. We dipped into the river of spirit together, sipping a cup of common experience, tasting God slowly.

Journal Questions
"Your God Will Be My God"

- How do you experience God in your own life?
- Nonverbally describe "your God"—with an image, colors, or drawing.
- How has your understanding of God changed through a friendship?

"Wherever You Die, I Will Die"

Dying takes many forms, and our bodies are engaged with dying all the time, whether we let ourselves know it or not. We also have the power to face death freely, as Ruth did. When we are not bound by the fear of dying, we are released to live fully: then death becomes the precursor to life, rather than the other way around.

Ruth's desert pledge promised loyalty even beyond the boundary of death: "Wherever you die, I will die . . . May Yahweh do this thing to me and more also, if even death should come between us!" (1:17 JB). For Ruth, the period between conception and the baby's birth must have been a time of hope and a time of dying to her old independent self. She was leaving the pre-pregnant separate individual person whom she knew herself to be in order to begin a lifelong connection with the stranger growing inside of her body. She would, in fact, allow the child to come between herself and Naomi. At the same time, of course, the child would solidify her relationship with Naomi.

Not only did Ruth have to face the symbolic death of her separate self, but she faced the actual possibility of death as well. There were real physical risks for her as an older woman bearing her first child. Although Ruth had a strong, healthy, farmworker's body, she lived close to nature and would have known the many dangers of childbirth. The mystery of death and birth were closely linked beneath a surface calm of this wintering period.

For Naomi, the question of death had a different meaning than it did for Ruth. Naomi was older, and she had already lost a husband and two sons. She was not the one at risk any longer, and she knew from experience that she could survive. This time it was Naomi's turn to accompany Ruth on a fearful and dangerous path, assuring her that she would protect the child if anything happened to Ruth. As winter friends, they could face the possibility of death without hiding from it or leaving one another.

Universal themes, especially the nearness of birth and death, pervade our winter relationships. To all outward appearances, the winter season is a time to be alone, to become a friend to one's own self. But as we do that, we discover the common core of our humanity—aliveness itself—mediated through the spirit of God. In silence we can approach the possibility of death and reflect on those mysterious inner forces that bring new birth out of death or collapse or tragedy. Time alone becomes time shared with others at the deeper level of wonder and mystery.

If we do not block our fear of dying or avoid the loneliness and despair that comes with certain winter seasons—what St. John of the Cross called "the dark night of the soul"—then we can participate in the dying of old forms, old relationships, and outdated patterns. With our winter friends, we can explore the inner terrain of the spirit and share the silent world of gestation as new life takes shape inside, before it is birthed in the world.

I have learned to trust that the intimacy of winter friendship can be shared with several people at one time. Silent retreat is at the core of our Seekers church community. Twice a year the eighteen members go on silent retreat together. We intentionally spend those weekends without words (except for what the retreat leader offers), sharing the experience of God's mysterious presence and closing with a celebration of the Eucharist. There is a sense in which we are *in God* together, as though we were sharing a womb-space. Somehow, silence is an experience of death. Like Naomi in Moab, we are stripped of individual preconceptions about God and about how our lives ought to be, in order to participate in creating the truth of how life can be. But those silent retreats are also the prelude to new life in our community. In silence we taste the new life of spirit together.

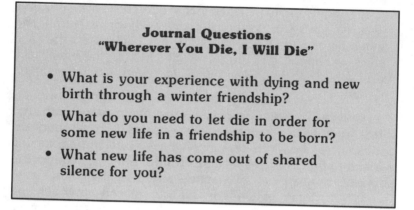

Journal Questions
"Wherever You Die, I Will Die"

- What is your experience with dying and new birth through a winter friendship?

- What do you need to let die in order for some new life in a friendship to be born?

- What new life has come out of shared silence for you?

7. Spring Friendship:
Birthing New Life

Naomi took the child and became his nurse
    in we-ness of spring
        after long waiting.

The women wove stories of new life:
    "The child
        will be a comfort
        in your old age..."
            Naomi renewed, reborn;
    "Blessed be Yahweh
        who did not leave the dead man
        without next of kin..."
           a family restored;
    "For Ruth
        who loves you
        and is more to you
           than seven sons..."
interpreting culture a woman's way.

The men kept account of the fathers:
    Boaz succeeded Elimelech and Mahlon
    (a redeemer inserted by Ruth and by God)
    as father to Obed...to David...to Joseph
        ...and to Jesus, fathered by...
        (another redeemer inserted by Mary and God).

Their record was clear,
    generations all named
    but they couldn't keep Yahweh contained.

Integration

Birthing continues to happen throughout life, both inwardly and outwardly. Friendships help the process by midwifing change, releasing the past, and welcoming the future. The image of a spring dyad—mother and child—is one of safety, nurture, and language. Between adult friends, safety becomes trust, nurture grows into mutual love, and language provides memory and hope. As the biblical story draws to a close, the images of birthing take on a community dimension as well as a personal level. Safety and trust produce internal integration; nurture and love invite new cultural interpretations; language and memory provide continuity.

The birth of Obed, whose name meant "serving," marked the final phase of the relationship between Ruth and Naomi. Long-awaited by Naomi, Obed *served* God's story in many different ways. He fed the hunger in Naomi's soul that could not be filled with food alone; he linked Naomi's singular decision to return to Bethlehem with the larger context of the covenant promise; he restored the family line; and he served the people of Israel as a sign of God-with-us instead of a God who just visited every so often. Indeed, Obed was the precursor of another babe who would be born in Bethlehem many years later from the same family line.

The story says that "Naomi took the child to her own bosom and she became his nurse" (4:16 JB). Figuratively, Naomi drew the child close to her own body; she became Obed's guardian, his home, and they became a primary pair. Naomi embodied the image of Yahweh as a great bird (2:12) as she drew Obed under her protective wing. Independent Naomi had been transformed by Obed's birth from a dried-up old crone to a productive woman again. Naomi took the child as her own, nursing him with love that was wise and mature.

When we picture Naomi as a mature woman beyond childbearing age holding the baby at her bosom, the biblical story provides a full metaphor of integrating different stages of a woman's life within the context of a female friendship. The multiple image of a nurturing elder like Naomi, a productive working woman like Ruth, and a newborn child like Obed is a symbolic triad, an internal image for us which carries the promise of creativity and meaning for women beyond having babies and beyond the childbearing years.

Naomi and Obed evoke a primal image of communion, of past and future, of chosen bonding forged through the commitment of friendship rather than simple biology. Naomi, as the wise older woman serves the child and, at the same time, the child serves to carry the woman's life into future generations. Naomi stands for wisdom and patience, vision and guidance, reflection and stillness, caring and the freedom to risk her life by choice. As the other half of the metaphorical image, the child means new life, new form in the world, dependence and need that can shape adult interactions toward compassion. The child symbolizes hope for the future and vulnerability in the present. Ruth's child in Naomi's arms is an image of their friendship through which each one experienced a new birth of trust, love, and hope.

With all the attention on Naomi and Obed at the end of the story, Ruth seems to disappear, as though she had completed her female task of marrying and bearing a son. However, Ruth's strong, loving presence in the on-going drama was recognized by the women of the village as they interpreted Obed's birth to Naomi, praising Ruth as the "daughter-in-law, who loves you" (4:15). Ruth had not disappeared from the collective consciousness of the Bethlehem women.

Nor had Ruth disappeared from the relationship with Naomi. But in the face of Ruth's original commitment to Naomi—that nothing would come between them—the child appeared as an interposer. A new kind of friendship between Ruth and Naomi would have to begin in order to include the offspring of their journey together, birth growing out of birth.

If the story had ended with Ruth giving birth to a son, it would have been a conventional story in which the younger woman "won" by finding a wealthy husband to father her child, and the older woman "lost" because she had outlived her usefulness once her friend found a man to marry. But in this biblical account, it is the dynamic *partnership* between Ruth and

Naomi which actually produced the situation in which Obed could be born. The two women were faithful in their commitment to each other, and the arrival of Obed was a sign of their fruitfulness, their creative energies. The dyad of Naomi and Ruth expanded by the child carries good news for us.

If we identify with Ruth alone—or Naomi alone—or Obed alone—we end up with an incomplete image of a woman's life. United, however, the two women and the child provide a complex metaphor of internal integration. Ruth's courage and self-sufficiency as she went to work in the fields provides an ancient image for our work in the world as strong, capable women. Naomi's determined hope for family and children holds out a model for believing in our visions. And Obed's long-awaited birth embodies hope for new life that will grow out of trusted relationships.

As mature women, we can bring the dedication of Ruth and the vision of Naomi to the creative work of birthing relationships and building community. Perhaps it is through our friendships that we can birth the message of promise for the future. The pairings of Naomi and Ruth, Ruth and Obed, and Obed and Naomi provide a biblical image for inner communion that is rich with generative possibilities.

Friendships provide us with new possibilities, either through direct experiences together or through stories about other times and other places. Through an older or younger friend, we can discover aspects of our lives that would have remained hidden otherwise. There is always a dialogue going on between outer experience and inner knowing or imagination. Within the context of a committed friendship, we can grapple with unrecognized parts of our hopes and fears on the path to wholeness.

Most of us enter adult friendship from a preferred stance, either as the independent Naomi, dependent Obed, or interdependent Ruth. Over time and experience together, we move around the triangle, sharing different seasons and taking on different roles with friends as we give birth to new levels of integration.

In my own life, I have usually begun a friendship from the stance of Naomi. As the eldest child in my biological family, there was not much space for being a dependent and needy child. In an effort to please my parents during the chaotic years of World War Two, I learned to "stand on my own two feet" and walk in the world as Naomi did. I have maintained that independent stance in friendship as we have moved from one Moab to another during Peter's Army career. I have always been cautious about committing myself to another woman friend as Ruth did.

But the friendships which have lasted over time have been those in which I could shift to Ruth's interdependent position, and eventually move to Obed's dependent role for periods of new birth. My relationship with my friend Marianne moved beyond independence when I went through a health crisis and felt helpless as a child during and after surgery. Marianne cared for me in her home because Peter was in Germany then. She provided safety and nurture as Naomi did for Obed until I could relax into her care for me. In my journal I recorded a madonna and child image that appeared in my dreams and my conversation during that particular period of crisis. Now I know that the vulnerable child in both Marianne and me has provided a core connection for our friendship, allowing us to move easily from Naomi's independence to Ruth's interdependence and Obed's dependence as one or the other of us gives birth to new levels of internal integration.

Journal Questions
Integration

- Identify the role that seems most natural to you at the beginning of a friendship: Naomi's independence, Obed's dependence, or Ruth's interdependence.

- Describe a friendship in which you have experienced all three roles over time and relate that friendship to your current sense of internal integration.

Interpretation

Birthing is never a complete break with the past: birthing always comes from somewhere. By describing the threads that join past and present, we can interpret events through the prism of new insights. A dialogue develops between inner images and external events, shaping our perception of personal truth, intimate relationships, cultural myths, and finally, our understanding of God. As we approach old age, the challenge of welcoming newness can be a sign of life itself. Alone, we may only be able to maintain an illusion of control and stasis. But in relationship with a friend, we can experience change with enough support to integrate what is new, uncontrollable, and beyond the boundaries of language or thought. While it is possible to give birth alone, we need relationships to extend that birth through time, integrating the present with past and future.

Like a collective mother's voice, the women of Bethlehem reflected the story of Naomi's spiritual journey from a woman's standpoint. They had once witnessed the promise of Naomi's spring marriage to Elimelech, followed by the summer emptiness of famine and her departure from Bethlehem. They had greeted her return with the searing question, "Could this be Naomi?" Then they had given Naomi a place to name her winter despair and had watched while the cycle of seasons began again: spring friendship with Ruth, summer searching for food, autumn acceptance into the village property structure, and winter waiting for the child. Now the community of women rejoiced once more in the coming of spring to Naomi's friendship with Ruth through the birth of Obed. The women of the village—not the village elders or scribes—named the child and provided interpretive language for Obed's role in the story.

The village women spoke for the collective womb-space of a people: they were the guardians of survival, the carriers of continuation, and the bearers of God's blessing. As they celebrated Obed's birth as a comfort to Naomi in her old age, they recognized that Obed was a sign to Naomi—and to the community—of being filled by God's promise, of being called into the future. Beyond the simple provision of food, God provided continuity to the family and thus fulfilled the promise of life for the community: "Blessed be Yahweh who has not left the dead man without next of kin this day to perpetuate his name in Israel" (4:14 JB).

Even though the women of Bethlehem upheld the traditional value of bringing children into the community, they were able to re-interpret the cultural preference for males and to celebrate the birthing power of friendship between Naomi and Ruth: "[She] is more to you than seven sons," they proclaimed (4:15 JB). By ascribing to Ruth more value than seven sons, the women were celebrating the birthing qualities of female friendship. They recognized Ruth's love for Naomi as the source of new life, and their blessing was a remarkable re-interpretation of official community values! According to the male value system, no woman could be as valuable as a son, let alone "seven sons." But as the women told a different story, their version became the biblical story, the carrier of God's truth. They re-interpreted the past and provided language for a new theology of life based on love more than law.

In our day, a community of women who can re-interpret our experience from a woman's standpoint can be a powerful field for our springtime birthings. Although we give birth individually, aided by the midwifing of a friend, the ability to find meaning and value for our lives depends upon the stories that link our birthings with a larger interpretive framework. Among women who understand that the biological urge to have children is, at the core, a drive to bring spirit into form, the celebration of bringing all forms of new life into the world is an important aspect of being female together. The women who help us name and interpret our birthings have a priestly function and express God's call to women beyond bearing children.

In my own life, the women's ministry of Faith at Work has again and again been a place to hear the Bethlehem song celebrating women's friendship. I have often come to a Women's Event as Naomi, with difficulty celebrating a woman's love as being more important than achieving status or control in the external world of work and material possessions—our equivalent of having "seven sons." Sharing my story with other women has helped me to look at the strands between my present experience, and internal voices from the past that denigrate intuitive and personal ways of knowing truth in favor of logic and control—our equivalent of the law. Even though I cannot always hear the interpretive song of the Bethlehem women celebrating the "love of Ruth who is more to you than seven sons," I know where to go when I have lost touch with that music. My ears are most open to hear a new song, a new interpretation of God's love, when a particular friendship has produced a new dance of life between Naomi and Ruth.

Recently I came to a Women's Event as just one more obligation on my crowded calendar. I had led the design for the event several times before and could not imagine that anything new would come from doing it again. I was also preoccupied with other things. Like Naomi, I felt full of responsibilities and empty of joys. The other women on the leadership team gave me a safe place to talk about the pictures I had brought from my childhood: my mother, sisters, and grandmothers. But the catalyst for change was Nan who came as a hard-working Ruth from a summer of providing for others: an extended family with grandchildren of different ages and her husband who was recovering from heart surgery.

Nan and I walked in the early morning hours, and she voiced her yearning for solitude, for space and time alone to face the next phase of her inner journey. We talked about the image of seasons in life and in relationships. As I listened to Nan, I felt myself shift from Naomi's role to Ruth's. I simply said, "I can walk with you. . .at a distance. . .so you'll have a winter friend and not have to take care of me, too." Somehow that was enough. I let go of my weary separateness for the loving interdependence of Ruth. The dynamic of the Women's Event, the words we shared in our small group, and the particular conversation that Nan and I had on our morning walk together opened my ears to the Bethlehem song anew. I could hear the pulse of life and name the value of women's friendship once again.

Journal Questions
Interpretation

- Where are the women who help you interpret the value of your own experience? (Consider books, media, friends, groups within your community.)

- Describe a time or season when you have heard their "Bethlehem song" interpreting facts with new meaning.

Continuity

Often the female version of a people's life is sung or told informally around the common activities of a household and is dependent upon an unbroken line of storytellers for its continuity. But written history—usually kept by men—often breaks that continuity, draining away the essence of life in an "approved" or "official" version. Stories that began as love are often codified as law; detailed records become the solidified form of women's dialogue.

The men of the city of Bethlehem, who were more concerned about family lines and property rights than about caring for two widows, contributed the final verses of the biblical narrative: a record of fathers and sons showing the connection between Ruth's son Obed and the genealogy of King David (4:18-22). In the details of those genealogy lists at the end of Ruth's story, we can find clues in the male system of records that support the women's story of how God works in the lives of ordinary people.

Though unnamed in the historical list, Ruth's place in David's family line, the "first family" of the covenant, is clear. But Ruth was a foreigner, one of the forbidden mates of the Old Testament: like many others, she did not fit the cultural image of pure blood-lines and covenant heritage. Ruth chose into God's plan before it became a matter of official record.

Through her commitment to Naomi—and to God, through Naomi's stubborn faith—Ruth became part of a long family line which included Tamar, Rahab, Bathsheba, and Mary, the foremothers of Jesus (Matthew 1:1-16). These women and unnamed others gave birth to hope because they chose life for themselves and their children with each generation.

As women reading the Bible today, we can marvel at the mysterious and creative power of God which refuses to be confined by the boundaries of law and language. Although the taboo against marrying foreign wives was based on God's directives to Moses, the stories of Tamar and Rahab reveal a creative God who was not confined by the Law. These women, including Naomi and Ruth, reveal a God at work in the world, creating out of the limitations of time, space, and finite being. This God brings life out of death through women who dare to take their own creative energy seriously.

God was being birthed in the lives of Naomi and Ruth beyond the confines of Bethlehem's archives. These two women dared to live as though their lives mattered to each other and to God. Their story together began with the barrenness of Naomi's sons, but the seed of Naomi's faith produced hope in Ruth, and ultimately, hope in a people. The women of Bethlehem were able to see that Ruth's love was a source of new life. As they incorporated the story of Ruth's love for Naomi into their cultural myths, the women provided an expansive view of God's intention and purpose in history. As part of the biblical record, the story stands as a parable of God's new birth through a female friendship.

In the end, birthing is an act of faith, a commitment to life. In the on-going history of the covenant people, the story of Naomi and Ruth gives birth again and again. As spring came to their relationship with the birth of Obed, birthing continued in ever-widening circles: the relationship between Ruth and Naomi opened the way to Boaz and Obed; the song of women in Bethlehem opened the way to a new interpretation of God; and the written record opened the way to God's larger plan for the birth of Christ.

When I think of ever-widening circles of birthing in my own relationships, I think of my friend Joanne whom I met on a church retreat nearly twenty years ago, during the winter period of Peter's second tour in Vietnam. Over the years, the commitment which she made to me at that time—the promise to share her home and her life with me every week—has taken on redemptive qualities.

When we were first getting acquainted, we used to stand in church and say these words: "We covenant with the Lord and with each other: to walk together in all His ways as He reveals Himself to us. . ." As when Ruth made that pledge to Naomi, Joanne and I could say the words of the covenant promise, but we had not yet discovered the meaning of walking together in friendship. Still, I felt the sheltering wing of God in her hospitality and found the safety, nurture, and dialogue of spring friendship as time went on.

Later, when Peter returned and we lived in Kansas, Joanne and I moved into a long-distance summer friendship. Charged by the polarities of our personality differences, she challenged my intellect with books and ideas from her years at Union Seminary, and I encouraged her intuitive side with my work as a potter.

When Peter and I moved to Washington, D.C., Joanne moved to Germany with her family and we decided to spend a month traveling together in Europe, an autumn community on the move. We learned the lessons of anger and confession and forgiveness in our travels—learned what walking together in God's ways could actually mean. Their children became part of our lives, and the six of us developed a sense of identity as a family cluster.

More recently, Joanne tasted the bitterness of winter as her marriage disintegrated and the girls grew up, leaving home for college. Peter and I opened our home and our hearts to Joanne as she tasted the loneliness of a dying marriage. In a new winter friendship she and I have been able to share a deeper underground river of spirit than we could when we first met.

Now spring has returned to our relationship, and new birth is coming once again. Sometimes I am in the role of Naomi, holding Joanne's inner child as she once shielded mine. Sometimes I love her like Ruth, "more than seven sons," and I re-discover my emotional depth as a woman. Recently Joanne wrote of her friendship with Peter and me:

> "As friends we have shared many of life's changes, transitions, endings, and new beginnings. When I feel stuck, they remind me where I've come from and that I have not always been nor will I always stay in this place. When I doubt, they remind me of things of which I have lost sight. When I celebrate, they cheer."*

Naming the history between us has been an important reminder that life is made of many seasons, that pain and death can be redeemed, and that spring will always follow winter. When we can see the continuity of the past, we can hope for the future. As the silent dialogue of our first winter season has been broadened and deepened by our experiences together, so the continuity of our friendship has become a source of God's comfort for aging and a promise of companionship for the spiritual journey that we share. We have indeed learned what it means to walk together in God's ways.

Journal Questions
Continuity

- Go back to the circle of friendship that you drew in chapter one. Add additional names of friends in each season, giving thanks for their differences and the qualities that they bring out in your life.

- Go back to the timeline that you drew in chapter two. Add symbols for new life that you see emerging, giving thanks for your power of birthing.

---

*Faith At Work News, Vol. 99, No. 2, Mar/Ap 1987.

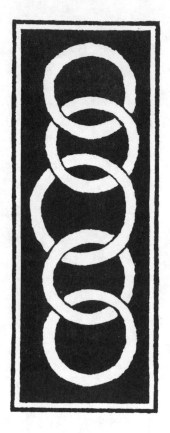

8. Seasons of Friendship with God

The spiral never stops.
Like seasons
     rolling toward each equinox
          we find ourselves
          anew with friends
re-birthing God again.

At first
     a muted sea
          surrounds us
     heard as heartbeat of the source
          infusing all
     with life —
the heart is home.

Then friends
     give birth to God
          by each one
     claiming
          what she needs for life —
               one ready to face death alone,
                    another ready to leave
               her mother's home —
          reframe a mother's love
     enfleshing God.

Come drought or simply growth
     inside and out
          the cozy pair
               gives way to search
          for call or form
     in work or words.

Discovery!
News!
    dry bones of thought, picked clean
    then blanched with brightness
light unsparing
    arid ideas

    soar

circling high above
the stony ground

    looking
      for signs of dampness
from a winter source.

If the seed of spring
    is dropped where summer heat
      and winter seep
can nourish roots
    that feed on deeps,

    then friendships grow to harvest

and the fruits of friendship keep us
through the dark
of winter
cold
    . . . until
      the daybreak comes again.

The Spiral Path

Today, we could simply dismiss the story of Naomi and Ruth as a charming tale of miraculous circumstances that resulted in the birth of King David's grandfather. But if we look at the deeper implications—at the nature of God revealed through this committed friendship—then we can focus the polarizing lens of the story on our changing relationships with God as revealed by the different seasons of Naomi's and Ruth's friendship. In their winter season, God was a protective womb, supporting new life until it could survive in the external world. In spring, God put a sheltering wing around them, providing safety for Ruth in the fields and for Naomi in the city. In summer, God seemed distant and hard, as though waiting for each one to risk safety and security for a larger goal. In autumn, God was manifested by the community with its on-going history and traditions. And then the cycle began again, describing the mystery of God in human experience.

We, too, can experience the presence of God through the special relationships that surround us, calling forth different capacities and different seasons over time. Like Naomi and Ruth, we must balance looking inward—for guidance or solace in the summer and winter seasons—with looking outward—for extroverted relationships in the spring and autumn seasons.

As an introvert, I feel familiar with the summer and winter seasons of friendship with God. I know what to do in those more internal times. I am more like Naomi than Ruth in temperament. I rely on tradition and past experience to claim my inward relationship with God which will keep new life rising again. In spring and autumn—the more extroverted and sociable seasons—I am surprised by God's love and care through others, as though I do not deserve to be included. Outward relationships bridge the isolation of individuality and claim the mysterious power of love.

Winter Gestation

A winter relationship with God begins with a simple decision to trust God's surrounding love and care, whether there is good evidence for it or not. The ability to do that may come out of life experience or stories that inspire trust, stories like the Exodus account or Naomi's journey, or from reaching back in our body memories to a time before birth when the womb provided a similar protective sea. The image of a surrounding and nourishing God as the infusing source of life exists both in biological memory and cultural myth.

Initially, Naomi understood the meaning of her life as a woman in a conventional way—through childbearing and family perpetuation. Her path seemed to be a linear one from birth to death, from springtime youth to wintry age. Her early spring years in Bethlehem were marked by a new home and family. Summer came with famine and the journey to Moab in search of food. Autumn, the period of establishing the community of an extended family after Elimelech died, was marked by the addition of Orpah and Ruth to her household. Winter came when her sons died leaving no children. According to the cultural myth, Naomi's life was finished in failure.

Then Naomi discovered the power of God in herself: she could respond to the urge for life or ignore it. Naomi chose life by embarking on a journey homeward, toward Bethlehem. She needed to complete the journey of individuation—the call to be creative throughout life—by reclaiming the faith of her past as an independent single woman. In doing so, Naomi had to draw on a spirit that went beyond what she had been taught, beyond the cultural belief which measured her value according to her ability to produce sons. Moving beyond Mosaic Law or Hebrew culture, Naomi discovered the mystical flame of God's spirit inside. Acknowledging the curse of childlessness which God apparently had put on her sons, Naomi was courageous and stubborn enough to risk a solitary journey because she dared to dream of being included in the covenant story once again. Naomi's choice for her *self* was part of a fuller revelation of God's love and intention for women.

Naomi began her journey to fill an emptiness in her soul, but she did not have to reach Bethlehem before God's grace began to show. God's accompanying presence was signaled by Ruth's commitment and the uneventful journey they made around the Dead Sea. Naomi's closed circle of seasons was opened by Ruth's unilateral pledge of companionship. Naomi said "Yes" to the possibility of relationship when she stopped trying to dissuade Ruth from joining her on the desert journey to Bethlehem. Like a woman discovering that she is pregnant in her old age, Naomi silently agreed to accept Ruth's presence and let it live within the circle of her wintry soul. By choosing to follow her inner sense of longing, Naomi provided leadership and direction for their friendship at a time when Ruth needed to follow, not lead. At that point, Ruth was ready to leave her past behind, but she had no direction of her own. Ruth needed Naomi's homing instinct.

Their winter friendship with God had begun with Naomi's decision to return to Bethlehem—a sheer act of will based on mute faith. At the point when all other sources of help and protection had been torn away, God provided them with sustenance for their long journey through alien territory. Like the Exodus story, God moved with them as spirit, unnamed but not unknown. With each step of the way, both women must have felt shielded, if not led.

In our extroverted and busy culture, there is little public attention given to the gifts of winter friendship with God. We purchase privacy; yet, on the whole, we do not like to spend long periods in quiet contemplation or alone. We flee from pain, despair, and even silence; we do not want those periods of introspection. We avoid discomfort and try to overcome interruptions; we want control over who will enter the gates of our city, or house, or circle of friends. Many of us do not even like to be reminded that conception is still a mystery, and childbearing itself requires a commitment to protect and nurture what we do not understand or control.

As women, we often avoid the inward journey of trusting God until it is forced on us by age or circumstances. A winter friend like Ruth, with courage to make a commitment without needing much response, may catalyze the shift from external questions of role and survival to internal questions of self and direction. In retreat from the activities of more extroverted seasons, we can discover the power to trust God in prayer, journaling, body-movement, or meditation. We may look death in the face and discover internal resources that we did not know were there. When we can live into the mysteries of a winter friendship with God, we may discover a surprising power to trust an inner spirit rooted in the core of "me," as Naomi did. We may discover the power to love without conditions, as Ruth did.

For me, the presence of God surrounds my *self* in the winter season, and is as close and supportive as the air I breathe. . . and just about as impersonal. Few people share my winter season of friendship with God: it is sustained by being alone, musing, meditating, walking, and wondering. I feel lost in darkness and inclined to self-pity. My dreams are infused by a river of spirit where images become shapes that move, shift, and reveal the state of my soul. Every morning I rise in the cold, silent house before dawn, sit with my journal to draw my dreams, wrestle with the lectionary readings, and pray for God's mercy as I read the newspaper. Periodic silent retreats ground me in this season, creating space within for new life. The weekly celebration of Eucharist or Communion is a reminder of my winter friendship with God, full of the mystery of death and life.

In winter, I am alone . . . quiet . . . introspective.

In winter, God is my silent source . . . giving me time and space to know and understand my *self*.

Journal Questions
Winter Gestation

- How would you describe your winter relationship with God?

- What activities nurture your winter friendship with God?

- What have you discovered about yourself and about God in different winter seasons?

Spring Encounter

The transition from gestation to birth marks the coming of spring in our relationship with God as it does between friends. Internal changes are revealed in external form, and there is new energy, activity, and hope. As we midwife and mother each other, we feel loved, nurtured, and needed. There is a sense of new possibilities of lightness and humor as we encounter the living God embodied in a human friendship.

Naomi and Ruth experienced the mutuality of caring for each other after they reached Bethlehem, and they encountered God's care as their needs were met providentially. Ruth faced into her fears of being molested in order to feed them both. Her willingness to risk her virtue—even her life—for the sake of their survival together evoked a blessing and a prayer from Naomi as they deepened their primary bond and did not seek a male protector. At that point, Naomi had the verbal connection with God through her Hebrew traditions, but Ruth brought a fresh experience of God through her actions. Together, they met a God who was close by, intimate, caring.

The differences in their age, energy, and expectations were the stimulus for reaching beyond conventional patterns for their very survival. One provided what the other needed, but neither was locked into the role of mother or child. Their needs met and joined to give birth to Ruth's daring choice to glean for their food. They shared their fears about Ruth's safety in the fields, and they rejoiced together over the serendipitous provision of Boaz and his generosity, a sign which Naomi recognized as God's parental care. Even the flirtatious bantering tone of Ruth's conversation with Boaz was, at another level, Ruth's encounter with God—trusting, easy, and comfortable.

There will be times in our lives when we need the mutual mothering that Naomi and Ruth gave to each other. We may reach for a friendship, a marriage, or a church home where we can feel safe and receive special attention and care. During those times, we may also look to God for nurture, shelter, and miraculous provisions. We will seek the active shepherding aspect of God instead of the mystery and silence of a winter prayer life. We will look for food and touch as a sign of God's parenting presence. A child-like quality may even add a dimension of playfulness to our spring friendship with God. We will want to feel welcomed and known and loved, not challenged or called to serve.

For me, spring is a playful season, full of freshness and tender starts. Even God seems full of good humor and puns in spring. It is the season of whimsy, of sharing my clown "Cheap Grace" with her feathers and bubbles at the hospital or at church, of knowing that I can be loved and accepted when I am a fool. But spring is the hardest season for me because I have the least control over myself and others. I cannot earn the joy that comes unexpectedly, surprisingly, as "good news" from the least likely sources.

The power of spring birthing is strong in our bodies and our souls. Like the image of Naomi holding Obed, we can claim the power of new birth beyond literal childbearing, in both aging and singleness. Birthing—physical and spiritual—occurs more easily with the affirmation and encouragement of a friend, either person or spirit. If we find a mutually nourishing friendship to midwife our births, we will continue to claim God's power of creativity through us until the very edge of death. If we do not have spring friendships to nurse the inner child of new life, then we may become the dry and bitter crone that Naomi thought she was when she arrived back in Bethlehem. We do not have to be ashamed of our dependent periods, early or late in life. Birthing does not last forever, but during that season we need warmth and caring.

Spring gives us an opportunity to follow our inner sense of purpose developed over the winter season, and to find an outward encounter with another loving person which expands our hopes and energizes creation. As we encounter God in the kindness and compassion of human caring, new understandings of God's "tender mercies" are born.

For me, spring is the season of grace and trust, of hearing Jesus call me by name to come as a little child—to get into the manger with Him and be cared for by Mary and Joseph. Some tiny detail of creation becomes a visible sign of God's grace: a special bird comes regularly to the feeder; the smell of fresh bread invigorates my walk to work; somebody sends me a cartoon that makes me feel special, noticed, and enjoyed. Little things help me know I am baptized into the family of God.

In spring, I am tender . . . fresh . . . new.

In spring, God is protective . . . generous . . . promising.

**Journal Questions
Spring Encounter**

- Where do you feel sheltered by God?
- How do you experience God playfully?
- Where do you feel challenged toward birthing?

Summer Call

A springtime faith is a good beginning for new growth, but it cannot sustain the fullness of our adult potential. The call to act independently and to claim who "I" am marks the summer season of friendship with God as well as with humans. If we try to hold to the spring image of God as a loving father or mother, we may resist moving on to the loneliness of summer. If so, we can expect to be pushed out of the nest—forced to fly. That, too, is good parenting.

A summer God calls us beyond the known patterns of family and community to be creators of new structures in society. A summer relationship with God is first marked by a personal sense of call, of special mission. In succeeding summers, our call may deepen into radical change of views toward institutional and cultural religion or a passion for social justice and prophetic vision.

Naomi's summer relationship with God began when she moved beyond the traditions of choosing the expected kinsman-redeemer, to choosing a man who embodied the justice and mercy she sought for Ruth and herself. When their food source dried up, Naomi let go of the nurturing support which God had provided for them. She dreamed a daring scheme for Ruth to undertake, risking everything to find a place for both of them with Boaz—a place where they would be treated with kindness and respect, as people instead of property. Naomi made a summer decision of determined will and then had to discipline herself to wait for results.

Ruth's summer relationship with God began as she chose to follow Naomi's instruction, to prepare for her initiate's task, and to approach Boaz with her specific request instead of simply receiving his freely-given attention. Ruth apparently trusted her internal sense of timing and the external field of God's presence for support in her lonely mission. She claimed the power of her whole person—body/spirit, language, and relationships—to confront danger and ask for what she wanted.

In their encounter Ruth and Boaz met each other as individuals equally valued by God. They were both able to move beyond the circle of conventional behavior when he did not tell her what to do, but asked instead, "Who are you?" When Ruth asked Boaz to risk his own reputation by circumventing the traditional order for being their kinsman-redeemer, Boaz agreed. He responded to her from his vulnerability—his age and his loneliness. By following his inner sense of love for Ruth and justice for the two women, Boaz opened the circle of Mosaic Law. In his response to Ruth—promising to do whatever she asked—Boaz found his own summer relationship with a God who was larger and more inclusive than tradition described.

The primary stimulus for an internal shift to summer is the question of finding individual expression in the world. We listen for a call that is unique. The dynamic tension between claiming one's self and relating to another keeps summer friendships on edge, stretching, reaching for excellence, or testing the limits that served as safe boundaries before. Mentors belong in this season. Challenging or critical competitors may also be summer friends. Like the encounter between Ruth and Boaz on the threshing floor, a summer friendship may contain hunger, fear, danger, and potential redemption. A summer friendship with God will feel the same—testing, challenging, stretching.

With a summer friend, we confront the powers that would make us conform to traditional patterns, and together we fight for a better future. If we can welcome these friends as the ones who quicken us to a larger vision for life, then we, too, can experience redemption—individual and corporate. Just as Ruth's action became part of God's on-going story, our separate actions for personal goals can become part of God's redeeming activity among humans on behalf of the outcasts, the marginal ones—the Ruths in our midst!

Summer is a season of change, of entering alien territory and risking life itself for some larger goal. We meet God face-to-face in the darkness, finding both name and mission—a place in God's story that is uniquely ours—and discovering the presence of God beyond the laws of society. We hunger and thirst after something more than physical food. We leave the safety of spring provision, forced by sources that no longer exist or simply by an internal readiness for challenge and independence. We seek new vision, new call, a change in the present order. We dare to act in new ways, to create new forms of justice and mercy in response to God's timing and internal gifts. Ideas and images materialize out of our solitary needs and give us courage to speak for others who have no voice.

As the season of call, summer fits my Calvinist soul. I like to work and to risk: it makes me feel competent and capable. I like to puzzle over God's call to vocation, examine my gifts, find a need, and *go for it!* I feel the urgency of God's vision for justice behind a dream I carry—a dream for the very old and the very young to minister to each other in day care centers in every church or fellowship hall. My forum is Faith at Work; my audience, people who come for conferences or retreats where I am asked to speak.

As the season of persistence and determination, discipline and focus, summer impels me to write and re-write, wanting to say what I mean in the fewest possible words. I wish for more flair and creativity, but often keep too busy for the playful activities that would encourage my imagination. I claim my gifts for interpretation, giving form and substance to things that others vaguely feel.

A summer relationship with God feels natural to me, as though the purpose of life is work, duty, and reforming society. But I know that working hard gives me the illusion of control, of being able to earn God's approval. I need the balance of the other seasons to keep from being a solitary, nagging critic.

In summer, I am restless . . . eager . . . searching.

In summer, God is probing . . . calling me to explore . . . inciting me to risk.

**Journal Questions
Summer Call**

- How do you experience God as a summer friend?

- Can you identify your call or vocation right now? Is your call different from the work you do for income?

- What risk or danger has been required in pursuit of your call?

Autumn Incorporation

As a communal counterpart to spring, autumn is the most difficult season for friendship with God in our individualistic culture. Most of us do not have the experience of an extended family or clan, and yet covenant community is the on-going expression of God in both Hebrew and Christian writings. The close-knit community of a church or rural village has largely disappeared from our culture, but the internal need for a larger field of relationships has not been eliminated. We still need to find a community in which to explore the diversity of God's intention for human life.

The people of Bethlehem gave voice to God's intention. Naomi's longing for community gave her the internal courage to initiate action even when the external signs of blessing were missing. But integration into the community was actually completed by the circle of elders who agreed to let Boaz be the kinsman-redeemer, and by the chorus of women who reminded Naomi that Ruth was more to her than seven sons.

Although the relationship between Boaz and Ruth broke the cultural desire for racial purity, and the relationship between Naomi and Ruth made the role of women's friendship more visible, the interpretive role of the community was essential for creating a new image of God's intention: redeeming the role of women and women's friendship in the language of story and song! The community's autumn relationship with God was celebrative and inclusive. According to their covenant tradition, the community itself was an expression of God's purpose in that time and place.

In autumn community, the multiple form of God's presence, we can expand our sense of purpose and belonging, share stories of how life is and how it ought to be, and catch sight of how memory and imagination can make life fun and interesting. Living with different generations can help us face our individual limitations of time and space, of death and violence. In community, we can develop a longer time-frame and participate in God's on-going redemptive purposes. In community, we can experience the fullness of God.

Autumn friends may be the nucleus of community. They can help us bridge the isolation of individualism and connect our lives with a variety of other people. With autumn friends, we can catch a glimpse of more permanent forms of community. Changes that have been taking place for us as individuals can be shared and confirmed.

We are social beings. We take our external clues about self-identity from the reactions of others. From the multiple levels of being known by autumn friends, we will get a more accurate, diverse, nuanced picture than we can provide for ourselves. One partner is not enough to mirror the complexity of any human personality. In the case of Ruth and Naomi, the village women were the ones who could name Ruth's devotion as more important than seven sons. They recognized that the friendship between the two widows had blossomed and borne fruit. The women could re-interpret the cultural myth that confined women to a childbearing role and could celebrate a whole new image of God—expansive, inclusive, and loving.

Today, a small community can help us diversify from the norms of society and, at the same time, provide security within the known conventions of communal life. Within a community, we can relax the exclusiveness of springtime pairings and expand the boundaries of family to include other casual and intense relationships from summer and winter. We can move from thinking in singularities to working in the broader functions of "our" life together. In belonging to a community, we can also face the truth that we are all outcasts, strangers, even outlaws. We can glimpse the rich tapestry of creation and recognize our need for others.

My autumn relationship with God is focused at Seekers, my church community. As a community, we are committed to team leadership with lay clergy and male-female polarities. We spend a good deal of time working with our gifts and the needs of people around us. When I am with Seekers, I can let go of the terrifying finiteness of my personal life and enjoy the on-going flow of lives that are linked in God's unfolding story of friendship with human beings.

Our weekly worship service is very participatory: different people preach and offer the liturgy. Our weekly mission group meeting provides four of us with a regular place to share stories of faith and discovery, and gives us time for planning the School of Christian Living as our corporate mission. Our monthly members' meeting gives us time to make decisions about our inward and outward journey together. We also gather for playing: singing, dancing, camping trips, play-readings, art projects, and celebrative meals. Together, we know that God is less concerned with efficiency than faithfulness. Together, we remember to watch for the widows and orphans, the imprisoned and the sick at the edges of our community. Together, we have rituals and liturgies that shape our common life in the direction of God's love.

In autumn, I am stretched . . . surprised . . . awed by the diversity of community.

In autumn, God is multiple and diverse . . . revealing new dimensions of wholeness—male and female.

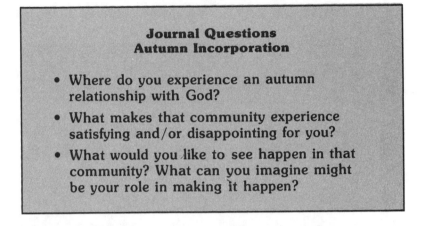

Journal Questions
Autumn Incorporation

- Where do you experience an autumn relationship with God?
- What makes that community experience satisfying and/or disappointing for you?
- What would you like to see happen in that community? What can you imagine might be your role in making it happen?

The Spiral Path Continues

The lives of Naomi and Ruth leave the center-stage of the biblical story in spring, with the birth of Obed. But the men and women of Bethlehem extend the story, integrating the child, Obed, into the story of their past—through Tamar, Rachel, and Leah; and into their future—through the genealogy of King David. . .and of Jesus. The genealogies stretch the story of Naomi and Ruth over time, describing a path in human history, carrying an Easter message of new life brought about by two individuals who dared to break through the covenantal restrictions and bear witness to a God of love and relationship.

As with the story of Naomi and Ruth, God extends our story, meeting us in every season, wherever we are, internally and externally. We have different types of friendships in each season, for balance and growth, for resolution and redemption, but the growth doesn't stop with the end of each season. While the path of seasons may be understood as stages of growth and development, the seasons continue to cycle by in a spiraling path, repeating the process and renewing us each time, building on the discoveries and relationships from the previous season.

The story of Naomi and Ruth—two women daring to claim their place among the covenant people—gives visibility to the creative image of God. If God is love, and we are made in the image of God, then loving is the purpose of creation. Life is for loving, and the pattern of friendships is the on-going experience of God's loving spirit among us.

Bibliography

Books have always been my friends, especially during the winter and summer seasons of my life. The books listed here have been particularly helpful in shaping my inner world so that the seeds for *Seasons of Friendship* could grow and mature. The list is not exhaustive; it is probably not even complete. But these are books you might want to read in order to fill in the gaps, follow the implications, and companion you on your own journey.

Bozarth, Alla Renée Bozarth. **Love's Prism**. Kansas City, Missouri: Sheed & Ward, 1987.

> *Bozarth's book is a poetic description of the basic theological issues underlying Seasons of Friendship. Chapter Four, "Loving Children," could be Naomi's song of aging. Chapter Five, "The Other Side of Love," is a celebration of the love that Naomi and Ruth discovered for each other.*

Bridges, William. **Transitions: Making Sense of Life's Changes**. Reading, Massachusetts: Addison-Wesley Publishing Company, Inc., 1980.

> *This is a well-written book with graceful and realistic descriptions of actual situations that mark modern life with many transitions. Bridges describes a resurrection pattern — moving from endings, to neutral periods, to new beginnings — that I found hopeful and helpful.*

Chernin, Kim. **The Hungry Self: Women, Eating & Identity**. New York: Times Books, 1985.

> *Associating eating disorders with the quest for personal identity by women, Chernin looks particularly at the separation struggle between mothers and daughters. Her clinical observations helped me formulate ideas about spring friendship and summer independence.*

Eichenbaum, Luise, and Orbach, Susie. **What Do Women Want: Exploding the Myth of Dependency**. New York: Berkley Books, 1983.

> *The authors suggest that because women are trained to be givers from the very earliest years, they need friends who see beyond the cultural myth and provide healthy companionship with mutual support.*

Fiorenza, Elisabeth Schussler. **In Memory of Her: A Feminist Theological Reconstruction of Christian Origins**. New York: Crossroad, 1983.

> *This book encouraged me to read the Bible with a "hermeneutic of suspicion" and an ear for the women's story behind the text. As the title suggests, many of the women's stories in the Bible have been forgotten or overlooked by theologians.*

Hammer, Signe. **Daughters & Mothers: Mothers & Daughters**. Bergenfield, New Jersey: New American Library, 1975.

> *This was the first book I read about the mother-daughter relationship which shapes so many of our attitudes about being a woman and relating to other women. The chapter on body and the separate self was particularly important in my understanding some of the issues for Naomi and Ruth at the beginning of their friendship.*

Hillesum, Etty. **An Interrupted Life: The Diaries of Etty Hillesum, 1941-1943**. New York: Random House, Pantheon Books, 1983.

> *Etty Hillesum has been called an adult Anne Frank because she, too, was a Dutch Jew whose life was cut short by the Nazis. Her diary records an extraordinary spiritual journey that prepared her to make a commitment (like Ruth's) which led to physical death. . . and spiritual birth!*

Keen, Sam. **Beginnings Without End**. New York: Harper & Row, Publishers, 1975.

> *This little book presents a seasonal pattern for life that was powerful enough to stay with me for ten years:*

Winter: Descent into Darkness
Spring: Ascent Toward Light
Summer: Rest and Ripening
Autumn: Toward the End of the Endless Way

I have drawn insights from Keen's images
without apology.

Keen, Sam. **The Passionate Life: Stages of Loving**. San Francisco: Harper & Row, Publishers, 1983.

> *Although Keen writes of stages, he really sings of a spiritual path that has an alternating rhythm between known forms and improvisation. He suggests that alternate periods of solitude and sociability keep us growing, and the point of these stages is to claim being made in the image of God as a lover. He helped me expand my own thoughts about relationships, beyond comfort or even companionship.*

Koppelman, Susan (ed.). **Between Mothers & Daughters: Stories across a Generation**. New York: The Feminist Press of the City University of New York, 1985.

> *An extraordinary collection of unconventional short stories by women of diverse racial and economic situations, the themes are critical to female friendship: sexuality as a mother-daughter issue in a patriarchal society, women's community as the matrix for identity, and life-cycle events as the key to exploring the issues of mothering beyond biological family.*

L'Engle, Madeleine. **The Irrational Season**. New York: Seabury Press, 1979.

> *Using the image of liturgical seasons to write about what it means to be human in relationship to God, L'Engle continues to challenge me with her images.*

L'Engle, Madeleine. **The Weather of the Heart**. Wheaton, Illinois: Harold Shaw Publishers, 1978.

> *L'Engle's poems make the drama of God's story come alive in biblical characters who live and love and struggle with relationships, as Naomi and Ruth did.*

McKenzie, John L., S.J. **Dictionary of the Bible**. New York: Macmillan Publishing Co., Inc., 1965.

> *A useful reference book with a Roman Catholic perspective.*

O'Connor, Elizabeth. **Cry Pain, Cry Hope: Thresholds to Purpose**. Waco, Texas: Word Books, 1987.

> *In this book from my mentor and guide within the community of The Church of the Saviour, O'Connor writes about her own struggle with call as it comes afresh in her mature years. Cry Pain, Cry Hope might well have been Naomi's story of coming home again.*

Rayburn, Carole, A. "Three Women from Moab," in **Spinning a Sacred Yarn: Women Speak from the Pulpit**. New York: Pilgrim Press, 1982.

> *This entire book of sermons has been an encouragement to me to write from a storytelling perspective. Particularly, Rayburn's sermon on Naomi, Ruth, and Orpah gave me an expanded view of their choices and pointed out their contrast with Moses.*

Rubin, Lillian B. **Just Friends: The Role of Friendship in Our Lives**. New York: Harper & Row, Publishers, 1985.

> *In this good descriptive book about the importance of friendship between women, Rubin notes the unrecognized and unritualized aspects, as well as the role of friendship in developmental stages.*

Russell, Letty M. (ed.). **Feminist Interpretation of the Bible**. Philadelphia: Westminster Press, 1985.

> *Other books by Letty Russell have been my theological guides in approaching biblical texts from a feminist perspective. This book, which she edited, is a recent collection of mature writers who continue to focus on the unfolding nature of God. It is from this stance of God's on-going revelation that I approached the story of Naomi and Ruth.*

Spencer, Anita. **Seasons: Women's Search for Self Through Life's Stages**. New York: Paulist Press, 1982.

> *In this small book with a seasonal image, Spencer sees youth associated with spring and aging with autumn, rather than viewing the seasons as a cyclical or spiraling image. She addresses the issue of women's struggles to achieve ego-autonomy in a patriarchal culture, and the need for social change if women are to have a working partnership with men.*

Trible, Phyllis. **God and the Rhetoric of Sexuality**. Philadelphia: Fortress Press, 1978.

> *Attention to word roots and the form of biblical texts always makes Trible's work provocative and enlightening. Her treatment of the Naomi-Ruth story in Chapter Six, "The Human Comedy," was an important starting place for me in writing* Seasons of Friendship.

Trible, Phyllis. **Texts of Terror**. Philadelphia: Fortress Press, 1984.

> *Again, Trible uses formidable scholarship to reveal the patriarchal bias behind the biblical texts. Of particular interest to readers of the Naomi-Ruth story would be the chapter on the concubine who is hacked into twelve pieces and*

*sent throughout Israel: a story which immedi-
ately precedes the story of Ruth and is set in the
same period and locale.*

Viorst, Judith. **Necessary Losses**. New York: Simon and
Schuster, 1986.

*A wise and witty book about what we have to
give up in order to grow up, her chapter on
friends is revealingly titled "Convenience Friends
and Historical Friends and Crossroads and
Cross-Generational Friends and Friends Who
Come When You Call at Two in the Morning."*

Marjory Zoet Bankson

Marjory brings a richness of life experience to her speaking and writing. As a graduate of Radcliffe College with honors in American government, Marjory completed her master's degree in history from the University of Alaska. She taught school and was the women's counselor at Dartmouth College before she became a full-time potter in 1970.

In the decade between 1970 and 1980, Marjory maintained a professional pottery studio while she explored classical spiritual disciplines and taught in the School of Christian Living at The Church of the Saviour, an ecumenical church in Washington, D.C., with six small congregations. Now a member of Seekers, one of the worshipping communities in that unique church, Marjory preaches regularly and continues to teach classes in the School.

Involved in the inception of the Women's Ministry of Faith at Work in 1980, Marjory has designed and shared leadership for many Faith at Work Women's Events. Since 1980, Marjory has been writing and speaking at denominational and ecumenical gatherings around the country.

Marjory studied at Virginia Theological Seminary (Episcopal) in 1984-85. In January, 1986, she was selected as the new President of Faith at Work, a nationwide ministry of experiential faith and renewal for the church. Since then, she has balanced her public ministry between writing and speaking to groups at the growing edge of the church.

Married since 1961 to Peter R. Bankson, a systems analyst with Synergy, Inc., the Banksons make their home in Alexandria, Virginia.

The fullness of Marjory's life journey, her capacity to feel and to see clearly, and her commitment to experiencing and sharing God in the world make her a woman with an unusual gift of re-interpreting past stories and re-kindling future dreams for all of us.

LURAMEDIA PUBLICATIONS

by Marjory Zoet Bankson
BRAIDED STREAMS
Esther and a Woman's Way
of Growing
(ISBN 0-931055-05-9)

SEASONS OF FRIENDSHIP
Naomi and Ruth
as a Pattern
(ISBN 0-931055-41-5)

by Lura Jane Geiger
ASTONISH ME, YAHWEH!
Leader's Guide
(ISBN 0-931055-02-4)

**by Lura Jane Geiger
and Patricia Backman**
BRAIDED STREAMS
Leader's Guide
(ISBN 0-931055-09-1)

**by Lura Jane Geiger, Sandy Landstedt,
Mary Geckeler, and Peggie Oury**
ASTONISH ME, YAHWEH!
A Bible Workbook–Journal
(ISBN 0-931055-01-6)

by Ted Loder
EAVESDROPPING ON THE ECHOES
Voices from the Old Testament
(ISBN 0-931055-42-3)

GUERRILLAS OF GRACE
Prayers for the Battle
(ISBN 0-931055-01-6)

NO ONE BUT US
Personal Reflections on
Public Sanctuary
(ISBN 0-931055-08-3)

TRACKS IN THE STRAW
Tales Spun from the Manger
(ISBN 0-931055-06-7)

by Elizabeth O'Connor
SEARCH FOR SILENCE
Revised Edition
(ISBN 0-931055-07-5)

LuraMedia operates as a creative publishing forum. LuraMedia selects, designs, produces, and distributes books, teaching manuals and cassette tapes with subject area specialization in personal growth using journaling, music, art, meditation, stories and creativity in a spiritual context.

LuraMedia is a company that searches for ways to encourage personal growth, shares the excitement of creative integrity, and believes in the power of faith to change lives.

10227 Autumnview Lane
San Diego, California 92126

LURAMEDIA ™